Allan M. Skinner

A Geography of the Malay Peninsula

and surrounding countries

Allan M. Skinner

A Geography of the Malay Peninsula
and surrounding countries

ISBN/EAN: 9783337292638

Printed in Europe, USA, Canada, Australia, Japan

Cover: Foto ©Andreas Hilbeck / pixelio.de

More available books at **www.hansebooks.com**

...STERN GEOG...

A

...EOGRAPH...

OF THE

...Y PENI...

AND

...NDING COU...

IN THREE PARTS.

PART I.

...LAY PENINSU...

BORNEO.

Edited by

M. SKINN...

Straits Branch of the R...

SINGAPORE.

1884.

SECTION I.

THE MALAY PENINSULA.

CHAPTER I.—General Description of the Peninsula,   1
        Physical Outlines,   2
        Political Outlines,   ... _   5
        Islands,   10
        Rivers,   10
      • Mountains, ...   11
CHAPTER II.—General Account of the Peninsula, in regard to its—
        Inhabitants,   11
        Products,   15
        Government, ...   16
CHAPTER III.—Details of the Northern (Siamese) Division of the
        Peninsula—
        General Description,   19
        Siamese States, ...   20
        States Tributary to Siam :—Kĕdah,   22
                Patâni,*   24
                Kĕlântan,   26
                Tringgânu, ...   28
CHAPTER IV.—Details of the Southern (British) Division of the
        Peninsula—
        General Description, ...   29
        The Protected States :—Pérak,   ...   35
                Sĕlângor,   ...   40
                Sungei Ujong, ...   42
        Independent States :—Nĕgri Sĕmbilan, ...   44
                Pahang,   ...   49
                Johor,   52
        The Straits Settlements, ...   56

* See Note at page 24.

SECTION II.

B O R N E O.

CHAPTER V.—General Description of Borneo,   61

Gulfs and Bays, Straits, Capes, &c.,   64

Dutch Settlements in Borneo,   68

English Settlements in Borneo—

Saráwak,   69

British North Borneo, ...   71

Labuan,   ...   72

Borneo Proper, ...   73

CHAPTER VI.—General Account of Borneo, in regard to its—

Inhabitants,   ...   74

Products,   ...   75

History,   ...   76

SUPPLEMENT.

CHAPTER VII.—A Brief Account of some of the principal Places

adjacent to the Peninsula, ...   79

CHAPTER VIII.—Outline History of British Connection with

Malaya.   81

LIST OF WORKS CONSULTED.

Encyclopædia Britannica, 1876-1883.
Straits Asiatic Society's Journals, 1877-83.
The Straits Directory, 1884.
Parliamentary Papers, 1874-80.
Wallace's Australasia, 1879.
Logan's Journals, 1846-61.
Crawfurd's Descriptive Dictionary, 1856.
Official Papers, 1874-84.

Maps and Itineraries (mostly unprinted) of the principal
Rivers on the East Coast :—

Tĕlŭng and Singgóra,...M. DELONCLE.
Patâni,	{ Mr. W. CAMERON.
	{ Mr. BOZZOLO.
Kĕlantan,	...M. MIKLUHO-MACLAY.
Pahang,	M. MIKLUHO-MACLAY.
	} Messrs. DALY & O'BRIEN.
	Mr. W. CAMERON.
Ĕndau, ...	...Mr. D. F. A. HERVEY.
Rĕmbau, ...	...Mr. D. F. A. HERVEY.

PREFACE.

THE want of a Book on the Geography of this part of the world, written in a way suitable for this Colony's Schools, has been frequently urged upon the Straits Government, and has led to the compilation of the present Work. Its scope is confined to *Malaya, Eastern Asia* and *Australia*— to those countries, in short, with which the Colony is principally concerned. It aims at affording such information about *Malaya* in particular, and *Eastern Asia* in general, as an English School-book, treating of Europe, would afford concerning Great Britain and the countries of Europe, respectively.

It is necessary to include some outline of the Geography of *India, China* and *Australia*; but it will be understood that a minute account is only given of the countries in *Malaya* and the more immediate neighbourhood of the Colony. The other Eastern countries—*India, China,* the *Indo-Chinese Continent* and *Australia*—have in turn been dealt with, in a relatively briefer and more general way. It has been sought to give, equally in both divisions, the latest and most authentic information.

The book is first of all a School-book, published in a form, and at a price, suited to those for whose use it is designed. But no attempt has been made to write down to the apprehension of children; or to break up the subject unnecessarily into special chapters of Physical, Commercial, Political, and General Geography.

It is hoped that, for educational purposes, an Eastern Geography, which has at any rate had the advantage of being compiled and edited in the East, may be of some use, even beyond the limits of this Colony. The position of Singapore is that of a city at the centre of a circle, which, having a radius of 3,000 miles, and embracing but one-fifth of the world's surface, yet, it is believed, contains more than half the population upon our globe; and an amount of commerce which is, at least, in proportion to its population : for Her Majesty's Possessions within this range have in themselves a sea-going trade of 251 millions Sterling, against 86 millions in the rest of the British Dependencies throughout the world.

The want of some such School-book as is here attempted is made clear in the fullest and latest of Geographical Text Books (KEITH JOHNSTON'S " Physical Geography " of 1880, London Series, 463 pages), in which the Peninsula is referred to in a single paragraph, while only 7 pages are devoted to all *Malaya*, and only 45 pages to the whole of the vast and important countries of the East.

In the other Geography-book of special importance for these parts—WALLACE'S " Australasia," 1879—*Malaya* is treated of more fully, but the Peninsula is not referred to at all.

The entire scheme of such a Work as has been sketched out above falls naturally into nine Sections, as follows :—

Malaya, *i.e.*, the countries comprised within a circle round Singapore of about 1,500 miles radius, treated in five Sections.

Other Eastern Countries, within a wider circle of about 3,000 miles radius, treated in four Sections.

It is contemplated to bring out these several Parts in a series of publications, and to arrange for their sale in three separate Parts, as follows :—

  I.—The Peninsula and Borneo.
 II.—Sumatra, Java and Eastern Archipelago.
III.—India, Indo-China, China and Australia.

The first of these is now edited at the wish of the Straits Asiatic Society. The countries of which it treats comprise all the British Dependencies in the Archipelago. To it, therefore, is appended an " Outline History " of our commercial and political connection with Malaya.

To make the volume as complete in itself as possible, a Summary is also appended of all the principal places in the East with which the Colony is concerned.

The heads under which each Part is treated will be in the following order :—

Description (including Extent, Physical and Political Limits, Mountains and Rivers, &c.)

Inhabitants (including Races, Tribes, Religions, &c.)

Products (including Industries and Commerce, &c.)

Government (including Administrative Divisions and History).

The use of the native geographical terms is avoided as far as possible. Wherever the term " mile " is used, the English Geographical mile (60 miles = 1°) is to be understood. The use of the word in other senses is confusing, and has, in fact, led to many inaccuracies, such as those noticed in dealing with the area of Borneo.

It must not be forgotten that special difficulties surround

the compilation of a School Geography respecting *Malaya*, and more especially the Malay Peninsula, as to which the best " reference " books afford but little precise information, and the Standard Works are, for the most part, out of date.

This particular volume could, indeed, scarcely have been edited yet, but for the special impulse recently given to the Peninsula's exploration by Governor Sir F. A. WELD, both through his own journeys in the Peninsula and the interest in the work which he has encouraged among others.

THE EDITOR.

Singapore, March, 1884.

MALAY PENINSULA

SHEWING SETTLEMENTS OF

SINGAPORE, PENANG, PROVINCE WELLESLEY,
AND MALACCA.

English miles

PÀRT I.

THE MALAY PENINSULA.

CHAPTER I.

GENERAL.

The Malay Peninsula, known to the natives as "The Malay Land" *(Tánah Maláyu)*, is the southernmost extremity of the great peninsular region of Indo-China, or Further India, to which it is connected by the prolonged Isthmus of Kra *(Kraw)*. In the narrowest neck of it, at River Pakshan, lies the South boundary of British Burma. To the South of Kra, the Peninsula projects for about 600 miles. It runs almost parallel with the northern end of Sumatra, and terminates at Cape Romania, *(Ruměnía)*, in latitude 1° 23′ N. Geologically speaking, the Asian extremity extends to Billiton *(Bilítong)*, and includes the three Archipelagoes of Bentan, Lingga and Banka, now cut off from the main. On the North, the boundary is British Burma ; and on the other sides, the Peninsula is surrounded by the waters of the Straits of Malacca and the Gulf of Siam. It gradually widens from about 40 miles at the isthmus to upwards of 3° of longitude, or about 200 miles, between the Dindings and Tringgánu ; and then contracts again to an average breadth of less than 100 miles in Johor. The area of the whole Peninsula, South of Kra, is somewhat over 70,000 square miles, being rather smaller than Great Britain, with an estimated population[*] of 1,200,000

---

[*] The estimate of 650,000 in the otherwise careful article on the Malay Peninsula in the new Encyclopædia Britannica, Vol. XV, 1883, is certainly much below the mark. The Colony and its dependent Native States now almost reach that number. Four of the items which go to make up that writer's total are *known* to be understated, viz.:—Straits Settlements, 314,000 (1881) ; Kělantan, 20,000 ; Johor, 20,000 ; Pěrak, 30,000, (*see* pp. 7-9).

souls, *i. e.*, about 15 inhabitants to the square mile. Of this whole number, 470,000, or nearly two-fifths, are found in the Colony of the Straits Settlements—a territory of 1,500 square miles, which, therefore, contains over 300 inhabitants to the square mile.

Physical.—The Malay Peninsula proper consists mainly of connected ranges of mountainous land, lying in the line of the Peninsula, which constitute a distinct water-parting between the streams flowing East and West to the surrounding seas. The western range continues unbroken from the interior of Kĕdah (6° N.) to the interior of Malacca (2° N.), and it re-appears at intervals in the South (Johor) and even in the island peaks beyond. On each side of the elevated region is a narrow littoral of recent formation, by which the Gulf of Siam and the Straits of Malacca are bordered, and which alone, it may be said, is inhabited and cultivated at present. The height of the mountain chain increases towards the wider parts of the Peninsula, at the back of the Dindings ; many peaks in Pĕrak being now known to exceed 8,000 feet—it is even said 10,000 feet : such as the Titi Wangsa hills between Kĕdah and Pĕrak, and Mount Robinson and other summits in the South of Pĕrak, which have only been ascended in the last few years. An unexplored ridge—Mount Tahan—on the East side of the River Pahang, near the West frontier of Tringgânu and Kĕlantan, is thought by the traveller MIKLUHO-MACLAY, who alone has traversed the interior (1875), to be the highest land of the whole Peninsula.

The entire Peninsula, to within some 10 to 25 miles of the coast, is broken and hilly, covered both on hill and plain with dense forests. It is of granitic formation, traversed by veins of stanniferous quartz and overlaid by sandstone, unfossilised clay slates, laterite, or ironstone, and in a few places, principally to the North, by limestone ; for although no trace has been found of recent volcanic action, there are several isolated and unstratified limestone masses, from 500 to 2,000 feet high, of a highly crystallised character, with no fossils of any kind.

The most remarkable feature, in a geological sense, is the prevalence of tin, as well as some gold and galena. The tin is found throughout the Peninsula, from Tavoi 14° N. to the Carimons (Kĕrimun) and to Lingga (on the Equator); and again, after a break of about 2°, as far South as Banka and Billiton (3° S.), which, as pointed out above, form, in every respect, but an extension of the Peninsula. Tin has not been found elsewhere in the Archipelago. The bed of the ore is, where it has yet been observed *in situ*, the quartz: which is found penetrating the granite at every elevation ; but all tin-mining has hitherto been confined to the deposits near the foot of the hills, in the alluvial ground, formed by the decomposition of the encasing rocks.

The primeval forests which, in general, cover the whole country, are occasionally interspersed with grassy plains in the North. The coast on both sides, and particularly the West, is almost invariably marshy and alluvial, scarcely raised above the sea, and, being under shelter of Sumatra, even and unbroken towards the Straits of Malacca. The seaboard is generally overgrown with mangroves for some four or five miles inland. In some parts the breadth of the plain reaches 30 miles, but it is usually much less. On the East coast, where there is an open sea, the hills at several points are close to the shore; but the general character of the country is the same on both sides.

The rivers are numerous, but, owing to the formation of the land, their course, though always more or less synclinal with the mountains, and therefore running southward—or, as on the N. E. coast, northward—is of no great length ; and their mouths are, in all but one or two cases, obstructed by bars or mud-banks. The largest are:—

On the East coast, the Pahang, the Kělantan and the Patâni; and

On the West coast, the Pêrak, the Běrnam and the Moar.

All these, and a few others, to a less extent, are navigable by light craft for considerable distances.

One peculiarity arising out of the rivers running rather North and South than East and West, is that in some of the principal points of the river system, the course of the streams running down from the same watershed, but falling into the sea on opposite sides, have their upper waters almost contiguous, *e. g.*:—the River Pahang and the River Slim in 5° North, and the River Sěrting and the River Moar in 3° North.

The climate is everywhere moist and hot, though seldom malarious, even along the low muddy banks near the coast. The mean temperature in the Peninsula is, throughout the lowlands of the plains, about 80°. There is, strictly speaking, no winter, nor even any very distinctly marked rainy season ; the alternate North-east and South-west monsoons distributing the moisture over the East and West slopes throughout most of the year. Except in some limestone tracts, especially in Pêrak and Kědah, the soil is not very rich : but is probably capable of growing almost every tropical product.

The average number of rainy days is about 190, and the mean rainfall of the Peninsula as a whole from 100 to 130 inches. The West coast is exposed to sudden squalls of short duration, known as "Sumatras" from the direction whence they blow; while the opposite side is closed to navigation during the North-east monsoon.

The *fauna* of the Peninsula, which is unusually rich, is allied, like the *flora* and the inhabitants, rather to that of the Eastern Archipelago than to the main continent. Here are the one-horned rhinoceros, Malay tapir, elephant and hog, all of the same species as those of Sumatra; also a small bear *(brúang)*, found elsewhere only in Borneo, as well as the Sunda ox of Java, besides two kinds of bison said to be peculiar to the Peninsula. On the other hand, the Asiatic tiger has extended his range throughout the whole region, even crossing over to Singapore and other adjacent islands. Of quadrumana, there are no less than nine species, including the chimpanzee, the kongkang, the black and white ungka, but apparently not the orang-outang.

Although the Peninsula has been coasted round by Europeans, and at a few places occupied by Forts and Factories, ever since the beginning of the 16th century : and although the interior is nowhere more distant than 100 miles from the sea, yet it still remains one of the least-known lands in Asia, and one of the few regions of which the greater portion can still be said to have been unvisited by civilised man. More correct surveys of its West side, however, have been pushed on in the last few years, and generally since the change in the administration of the Pêrak and Sĕlângor States (1874).

Political.—The Peninsula may be considered as politically divided between Great Britain and various groups of self-governed States, more or less under the protection and influence

of either Great Britain or Siam. In about a quarter of its
extent to the South, it is broken up into a number of quasi-
independent Malay States, which, if not tributary to, are yet
bound in Treaty with, the British. The influence of Siam
extends over the whole of the northern section, coming as far
down on the East side as about $4°\ 35'$ N. (the North frontier of
Pahang). A line drawn from this point North-west, along, and
some miles inland of, the East coast, and then across the
Peninsula to the Kĕdah Peak on the West coast ($5''\ 40'$ N.),
will thus define approximately the southern limits of all the
land more or less tributary to Siam. The rest of the Peninsula, which may fairly be styled the British portion, is occupied :—

> by the British possessions, grouped under the collective
> name of the " Straits Settlements;"
>
> by the large Protected States of Pérak, Sĕlàngor and
> Sungei Ujong on the West coast, which are now in
> effect under British administration ; and
>
> by the more or less independent Malay States proper,
> which can also be regarded as forming part of the
> British protectorate over the whole South of the
> Peninsula.

The northern portion contains nearly 40,000, and the British
portion to the South nearly 35,000 square miles. Although the
area of the former is greater than the latter, it contains only
about one-third of the population, and a still smaller share of
the commerce of the Peninsula.

Subjoined is a summary of the States comprised in these
political divisions, proceeding on both coasts from the North.

NORTHERN (SIAMESE) DIVISION.

STATES MAINLY SIAMESE.

Ligor, Sènggòra, &c.—Comprising altogether some 15 separate provinces mainly Siamese and Chinese, and including the South part of the isthmus of Kra, between 7° and 10° N., with a coast-line of about 200 miles on the East and a little more on the West side ; area about 17,000 square miles ;* population variously estimated from 150,000 to 500,000.

MALAY STATES TRIBUTARY TO SIAM.

Kĕdah, between Ligor and Pèrak, 7° to 5° 35′ N., with 100 miles on West coast ; area 4,000 square miles ; population probably exceeds 100,000.

Patáni and *Rĕman, &c.,* nine small States or Provinces lying between Sĕnggòra and Kĕlantan, 7° to 6° 20′ N., with coast-line on East side of 50 miles ; area (exclusive of all Pèrak valley), 6,000 square miles ; population about 50,000.

GUARANTEED MALAY STATES.†

Kĕlantan, between Patáni and Tringgánu, 6° 20′ to 5° 40′ N., 60 miles coast on East side ; area 7,000 square miles ; population large, variously estimated between 100,000 and 200,000.

Tringgánu with *Kĕmáman,* between Kĕlantan and Pahang, 5° 40′ to 4° 35′ N., with about 80 miles of coast-line on the East side ; area 4,000 square miles ; population about 20,000.

SOUTHERN (BRITISH) DIVISION.

The Colony of the Straits Settlements.—Penang including Province Wellesley, and the Dindings ; the territory of Malacca

---

* Throughout the Peninsula, the area can only be computed approximately, the boundaries not having been surveyed ; and it is only in the Colony and Pèrak that the population has been ascertained by enumeration.

† Treaty with Siam of 1826 (Art 12).

with Naning ; and Singapore, which is the capital, not only of the Colony, but, it may be said, of the whole Peninsula. These possessions, grouped together, go by the collective name of the " Straits Settlements," and now form a Crown Colony, containing about 1,500 square miles, and 470,000 inhabitants (1884).

PROTECTED STATES.

Pērak, between Kĕdah and Sĕlângor, 5° 10' to 3° 45' N., with about 90 miles coast-line on West side; area (including all the watershed of the River Pērak), about 8,000 square miles ; population almost exactly 100,000 (1883).

Sĕlângor with *Klang*, between Pērak and Sungei Ujong territory (since the 1877 boundary was fixed), 3° 45' to 2° 40' N., with a somewhat greater extent of coast-line on the West side than Pērak; area about 5,000 square miles; population about 50,000.

Sungei Ujong, a much smaller State, lying in the same basin, to the North and West of the Linggi River, and not separated from Sĕlângor by any well-defined natural boundary. Area, including the districts of *Lûkut* and *Sungei Rûya*, which now lie within its boundary (since 1877), about 500 square miles. Population about 14,000.

Of all the Malay States, the most important at the present time are probably these three Protected States on the West coast, which comprise about 13,000 out of the 35,000 square miles in the British section of the Peninsula. Since they have been brought under the influence of the Colonial administration, they have become most prosperous, and have now a population of about 13 to the square mile ; that of the rest of the Peninsula, apart from the Colony, being scarcely 8 to the mile.

Jělěbu, Sri Měnanti or *Hûlu Moar, Jěmpol, Rěmbau, Johol*
with *Jělei* or *Inas.* These five inland States, lying between
2° and 4° N., formerly constituted, with *Sungei Ujong* (now
protected), *Klang* (now part of Sělângor), *Naning* (now
Malacca territory), and *Sěgâmat* or *Moar* (now part of Johor),
the so-called Něgri Sěmbilan, or " Nine Countries," governed
by elective Pěnghûlus, or Chiefs, and titular Princes feudatory
to the Sultans of Měnangkâbau in Sumatra. The States are
now bound in treaty with the Colony. They surround the
Malacca territory, lying between Johor on the East, Pahang
on the North, and Sungei Ujong and Sělângor on the West and
North-west. Total area probably not more than 2,000 square
miles ; population about 30,000. The more important at
present are *Rěmbau, Sri Měnanti* and *Johol.*

_____

Johor (Jěhôr),* southern extremity of the Peninsula, from 2°
40′ N. to Cape Romania ; area about 8,000 square miles ;
population about 100,000.

This State (which now includes *Moar*) has, owing to its fine
situation, political and geographical, a unique position among
the Malay States. Though under the independent administration of its own prince, now called "Maharâja," its proximity
to Singapore ensures it adequate security. Hence it possesses
a large Chinese population, and a considerable revenue.

Pahang, between Johor and Tringgânu, 4° 35′ to 2° 40′ N.,
with about 120 miles of coast on East side ; area approaching

* The States below this line, like those of the Northern (Siamese) Division (p. 7) placed
below a similar line, enjoy full independence in their internal administration, though under some Treaty constraints.

10,000 square miles; population about 50,000. It is traversed by the longest and one of the most important rivers in the Peninsula, though too shallow to be navigable by any but small craft.

Islands.—The Peninsula's northern seaboard has several small islands, and insular groups, which lie in clusters of innumerable small islets, on both sides of the isthmus to the North. The coast further South is remarkably free from islands. The only ones of any consequence are Junk Ceylon *(Ûjong Sâlang)*, Lĕngkâwi and Penang *(Pinang)*, on the West side; the Carimons *(Kĕrîmon)*. Singapore *(Singapûra)*, and the Bentan and Bulang Archipelagoes, at the South extremity; and on the East side, off the coast of Johor, some high peaks, of which Tiûman and Tinggi are the largest, and a similar but less important group (the Great and Little Rêdangs) off Kĕlantan.

The large island or peninsula, Tĕntâlam, lies to the North of Sĕnggôra, in a situation which corresponds to that of Junk Ceylon on the West coast.

Rivers.—The Peninsula's principal streams, following the coast from N. to S., are as follows:—between the Pakshan (the lower course of which separates the Peninsula from Tenasserim in British Burmah) and the Rivers Mûda and Krîan, there are none but small streams. The first large river is the Pĕrak, with its chief tributaries—the Plus, Kinta, and Batang Padang. [The Pêrak, on the West, and the Pahang, on the East slope, are the largest river basins in the Peninsula, each draining an area of 4,000 to 6,000 square miles.] The other chief streams are the Bĕrnam, with as large a volume of water, but draining a less area; the Sĕlângor, the Klang and the

Langat on the South-west coast; the Linggi, the Moar, and the Johor, of which the estuary faces Singapore. On the East side, there is the Endau, the Pahang with its large tributaries—the Bĕra, the Triang, the Jĕlei, &c.—the Kwantan, the Bĕsut, the Kĕlantan with its large tributary the Lĕbih—and the Patâni.

Mountains.—The highest mountains of the Peninsula are probably not yet discovered. Those known are:—Kĕdah-Peak (Jĕrei), 3,894 feet ; Mount Titi Wangsa, 6,840 feet, between Kĕdah and Pĕrak ; Inas, in Kĕdah, 5,000 feet; Bûbo, 5,650 feet, and Ulu Tĕmĕling, 6,435 feet, near the right and left banks respectively of the Pĕrak river; the Slim range, 6,000 to 7,000 feet, in South-east Pĕrak; Mount Robinson (Riam), about 8,000 feet ; Chimbĕras, 5,650 feet, in Sĕlângor; Bĕrĕmbun, about 4,000 feet, in Sungei Ujong; Mount Ophir (Lêdang), 4,200 feet, until recently supposed to be the highest point in the Peninsula ; and Blûmut, 3,200 feet, in the centre of southern Johor, and where the River Johor takes its rise.

CHAPTER II.

INHABITANTS, PRODUCTS, GOVERNMENT.

INHABITANTS.

Races.—The inhabitants of the Peninsula, apart from the Chinese, Indians and other recent settlers, who now form nearly half its population and number at least 550,000, belong to three distinct stocks—the Thai (Siamese) numbering 150,000, the Malay 500,000, and the Negrito about 20,000.

The Siamese of pure blood, and the Malayo-Siamese, or Sam-Sam, occupy the territory from the isthmus to the confines of Kĕdah and Patâni, or as far South as about 7° of North latitude. The pure Siamese, to the North of latitude 8°, are the same stock as in the rest of Siam, and, like other Siamese, are Buddhists. The mixed race of Sam-Sam are, on the other hand, outwardly Siamese in feeling and religion ; but as to language they are as much Malay as Siamese, being true bi-linguists. In their traditions and customs, the Sam-Sam mostly follow their Siamese ancestry.

The main part of the Peninsula, below about 7° of North latitude, may be regarded as essentially Malayan. It is scarcely possible that the Malays can be really indigenous in the Peninsula; but whether they were originally intruders from Sumatra, or Java, or the neighbouring Archipelago of Rio, is a question still discussed by ethnologists. It seems most probable that the Malay stock, which originally peopled the kingdoms of Singapore and Malacca, and overspread the East and West coasts, came northward from the South of Sumatra (Palembang) by way of the Lingga and Rio Archipelagoes. It is certain that, within recent times, there has also been a steady flow of immigrants, subsequent to and independent of this earlier one, from a populous plain in the hilly country to the North of Sumatra, called Mĕnangkâban. This immigration, across the narrowest portion of the Straits, has been chiefly directed towards Rĕmbau, and the other small States to the interior of Malacca.

The whole of the mountain regions, all down the centre of the Peninsula, are and it may be supposed have always been occupied, not by the civilised Malay, who keeps to the coast and to the larger rivers, but by wild tribes of Orang Bĕnûa, or " men of the soil"—called, to the North of the River Pêrak, Sĕmang ; and to the South, Sâkei; and by a variety of other names in other parts. Their origin can only be conjectured ; but throughout the country, and especially in the South, their type is now essentially Malayan, and they differ from the Malay in religion and customs rather than in blood or language. They have, in fact, been described as " Malays unconverted to Islam ;" but those who have most carefully studied the question of their origin consider this description to be, ethnologically speaking, inadequate. The scientific traveller MIKLUHO-MACLAY speaks with the authority belonging to the only European, it is believed, who has lived among the various tribes in all their principal resorts. He travelled from South to North of the Peninsula during 1874-5 ; and his general view of these aborigines is expressed in the following note. The careful philological enquiries of Mr. J. LOGAN before that date, and the comparison of various vocabularies since collected by the Straits Asiatic Society, appear to support his opinion, so far, at any rate, as concerns a common pre-Malayan language * :—

" 1st. (There is a) connection between the various tribes of the Orang " Sâkei, living quite cut off from one another, in Pahang, Kĕlantan and " Sĕnggôrn :—

" 2nd. Some relation in point of language between the very mixed " and distant-dwelling Orang Utan of Johor with the Orang Sâkei in " the North of the Peninsula :—

" It is undoubtedly an interesting result to have ascertained that

---

* This passage is quoted from Journal No. I, p. 43, of the Straits Asiatic Society.
The other references here made are to LOGAN's Journals, Vols. I and II, and Straits Asiatic Society's Journals, Nos. 4-8.

"these tribes, isolated and ignorant of each other, are, throughout the
"whole peninsula from Johor to Ligor (South of Siam), thus closely
"connected in speech. This circumstance gives me a fresh conviction
"that my opinion expressed in the beginning of this year (1875) and
"before my second journey, is correct, viz., that the Órang Ûtan of
"Johor, notwithstanding their great intermixture, undoubtedly show
"traces of a *Melanesian* blood."

The whole number of these tribes is certainly not more, and probably
somewhat less, than 20,000 at the present time; and they are diminishing
every year, as a race distinguishable from the Malay.

The Malays, though probably not the most important original factor
in the indigenous population of the Peninsula, are by far the most important of the three stocks above-named at the present time. Under the
influence, first of the Hindus, and afterwards of the Arabs, the Malays have
developed some sense of national life and culture, and have founded
more or less powerful political States, in various parts of the Archipelago.
The common view of the Malay as a sea-rover is, now at any rate,
incorrect: the great majority of the Malay race in the Peninsula, as in
Sumatra, being engaged in agricultural pursuits.

The Malay language, here as elsewhere, is the accepted medium of
intercourse between the Peninsula-born settlers of all races.

Numbers.—The whole population of the Peninsula, including
settlers as well as the indigenous people dealt with above, is probably
under-stated at 1,200,000. On the basis of the last Census (1881), the
Colony alone numbers 470,000 (423,384 *plus* three years' increment
46,616), and, including the three Protected States, must certainly exceed
600,000.

The population of the Peninsula may be roughly distributed among
the various races as follows:—

Siamese Division,	Siamese,		100,000
	Mixed Siamese, ...	...	50,000
	Tributary Malays,	...	150,000
	Wild Tribes, ..	..	10,000
	Chinese, .		90,000
			400,000

British Division,	Malays,		350,000
	Wild Tribes,	..	10,000
	Chinese, ...	...	300,000
	Indians, ...	...	40,000
	Miscellaneous (chiefly in the Colony), ...	...	100,000
			800,000

Some pains have been taken to arrive at an approximation in these
figures; but, in the absence of any Census returns, outside the Colony,

they must be taken as showing the proportions, rather than the exact numbers, which probably exceed these totals.

The enumeration of the Malays and Chinese at the Colony's last Census (1881) gave precisely the same number for each race, viz. :— Chinese, 174,327 : Malays, 174,326. In the Native States it is certain that the Malays out-number the Chinese; and therefore the Malay race is still first in the Peninsula, so far as regards numbers. But to judge from the advance made by the Chinese in the Straits at the last Census, these latter will soon take the lead in numbers, as they have done for some time in most other respects.

Religion.—The Malays, including even some of the border Sam-Sams in the North, universally profess the Mahomedan religion. Until about the year 1250, they were pagans, or followed some corrupted form of Hindu idolatry. Sultan Mahmed Shah, who reigned over the Malacca dominion in the 13th century, was the first Prince who adopted the Mahomedan faith, and spread it during his long reign of 57 years. His rule extended over the neighbouring islands of Lingga and Bentan, together with Johor, Patani, Kedah and Pèrak, on the coasts of the Peninsula, and, it is supposed, over several districts in Sumatra. The adoption of Islam thus spread rapidly in the Peninsula; and the Portuguese found all Straits Malays were of that faith at the beginning of the 16th century, while a large portion of South-east Malaya still remained pagan.

Language.—The Malay language is the most important of the many dialects composing the Malayan section of the Malayo-Polynesian class of languages. The area over which it is spoken comprises the Peninsula of Malacca with the adjacent islands (the Rio-Lingga Archipelago), the greater part of the coast districts of Sumatra and Borneo, the Moluccas, the seaports of Java, and, to a less extent, those of Celebes, &c. It is the general medium of communication throughout the Archipelago, from Sumatra to the Philippine Islands; and it had already become so nearly 400 years ago, when the Portuguese first appeared in these parts. There seems, before that time, to have been no such written language as would correspond with the wide extent of spoken Malay: and no monumental records have been found with inscriptions written in Malay, before the adoption of the Arabic character.

It is the more remarkable that Malay, of all the Sumatran languages, should have possessed no writing of its own, since the Rejangs, Battaks and the Bugis in Celebes possessed, and still use, an indigenous character, said to be Cambojan in type. With the Mahomedan conversion, the Perso-Arabic alphabet was introduced among the Malays. Malay is essentially, with few exceptions, a dissyllabic language. From the Hindus, who appear to have settled in Sumatra and Java in the 4th century, the native populations received into their language a very large number of Sanskrit terms: and since the 13th century, a large number of Arabic terms have crept in through the religious influence of Islam. No real distinction can be made between *High Malay* and *Low Malay*, as with

Javanese and Kawi. *Low* Malay is no separate dialect at all, but a mere medium of intercourse between natives and Europeans.

Malay is probably spoken with greatest purity in the Rio-Lingga Archipelago, and among the Malay States in the S. W. of the Peninsula.

Character.—A general character can hardly be assigned to a people so widely distributed. That the Malays belong to the Mongolian division of mankind, is well illustrated by the strong resemblance between some of the higher types of each. The Malay head varies from the lowest type of coarse Mongolian, with a Negro tendency, to the finest form which the Turanian skull can assume without ceasing to be Turanian.

Nearly all Malays have thick coarse black hair, with weak and scanty beard, when it is not, as almost invariably, plucked out by the roots. The inhabitants of the Peninsula are well-mannered and even courteous; but of an undemonstrative disposition, betraying a certain reserve, diffidence and even shyness, which has induced many to suppose that there must be some exaggeration in the current account of the Malay's blood-thirsty nature. Coarse play is especially repugnant to them, for they are extremely sensitive on all points of etiquette and of encroachment on their personal freedom. Under generous treatment, they are gentle, docile and faithful; but although normally impassive and indolent, their passions are easily roused when wronged, and are liable to the frenzy which ends in that wild atrocity known by the name of running amuck, from the word "amok," (attack).

PRODUCTS.

Vegetable.—Of vegetable products, the Peninsula contains a host of trees, the timber of which is adapted for house and ship-building; canes and rattans, with which the jungles abound; and the cocoa-nut, areca, sago and gomuti palms. The most important products of the jungles are camphor and many varieties of gutta percha (*gĕtăh*). The nutmeg, cinnamon and clove have been introduced, and, except for a leaf disease in the nutmeg, thrive well.

The Chinese have introduced the cultivation of indigo, gambier and pepper, and the Europeans of sugar-cane, tea, tapioca and coffee. Rice and other kinds of grain grow well, but not in quantities sufficient for home consumption; and supplies are, therefore, imported from Java, Saigon, Siam, and Rangoon.

Mineral.—Tin is by far the most important of all the minerals found in the Peninsula, and all the more so because it is not found elsewhere in the Archipelago. The whole country has been described as "a vast magazine" of this rare metal; and it is now admittedly the most extensive tin-country in the world. Tin is worked at present in about twenty different localities on both sides and throughout the length of the Peninsula. The principal mines at this date are those of the Siamese provinces in the North-west, Intan, Sĕlāma, Lārut, Kinta, Kwāla

Lumpur, Sungei Ujong, Pahang, Kĕlantan and Patâni. Gold is found in several places, generally speaking the same as those above-named for tin. The principal is Jĕlei in the interior of Pahang, the gold of which brings a higher price by 3% than the best Australian gold. Other places are Chĕndras, Tâong (near Mount Ophir) and Kĕlantan. Rich galena ore occurs in Patâni. Silver has not been certainly found anywhere, except in this form. Iron ore is even more abundant than tin, especially throughout the South of the Peninsula. It has not hitherto been worked, as it is in Sumatra. Coal has, it is said, recently been found to the South of Kra, and some traces of it in Pĕrak and other places; but it is not yet worked in any part of the Peninsula.

Animals.—Elephants still abound in great numbers; the one-horned rhinoceros, Malay tapir, wild hog, the royal and the spotted black tiger, a small bear, the Sunda ox, two kinds of bison (said to be peculiar to the Peninsula), the musk-deer and several other kinds of deer.

GOVERNMENT.

Administration.—The only forms of government to be found in the Peninsula, outside the Colony of the Straits Settlements, are either tribal and elective, as in Rĕmbau and the contiguous inland States, or autocratic and hereditary, like those of the Malay or Siamese Râjas and Governors on the seaboard. Something of a tribal form of rule is to be traced in all Malay administrations; and none of them, whatever the form, appear to be " free" States, in any true sense of the word.

The government of the Colony is that of the usual " Crown Colony " type, Penang being represented in the Legislative Council, which sits at Singapore.

The administration of the three Protected States is unique, and peculiar to themselves; and, in its existing form, can hardly prove permanent. It has been a natural development from the state of things which was left after the military occupation of 1875. Supreme power is vested in a State Council, of which the Resident is the moving spirit, though it is presided over in Pĕrak by the Regent in person, and consists in each State of the highest native authorities as well as the principal English officials. The Residents are directly under the Government of the Straits Settlements, and have, of course, almost the entire control of, and responsibility for, the affairs of the State in which they reside. A royalty on the export of tin, in addition to the duty levied on opium, as in the Colony, contributes largely to the growing revenue of all these Native States.

History.—Singapore is the earliest of the Malay Settlements which can claim any history. The *Sĕjarah Malâyu* and other Malay annals represent " Singapûra " (which is known to have been on the same site as the present city) as having been peopled, not from Mĕnangkâbau, as is generally supposed, but from the neighbouring island of Bentan, which had a considerable maritime population when SANG NILA UTAMA, a chief of Palembang, settled there, and married a daughter of the Queen. This is said to have been about A.D. 1160.

The Johor Archipelago was probably inhabited from a very remote period, anterior even to the existence of any of the Malay race in Sumatra, by a maritime branch of the same people, radically Malayan, who are now found in the interior of the Peninsula and of the southern half of Sumatra. Several tribes in various stages of civilization still possess the Johor islands. Though little known to Europeans, they can never have been without Malay or Hindu-Malay visitors, for it was by the great rivers of Palembang, Jambi, Indragiri and Kampar, before whose embouchures these islands lie, that the Hindus of Ceylon and southern India must have gradually carried civilization into the interior of southern Sumatra. The Indragiri, in particular, appears to have been crowded with Hindu-Malay settlements, many of the numerous villages on its banks retaining purely Hindu names to this day. It was by this river, probably, that they reached the fertile plain of Menangkábau. It is probable that the Malays on these rivers had attained a certain civilization in advance of the wandering mountain tribes, even before the Hindus came.

That the ancient Singaporeans were of a maritime and not an inland agricultural race, may be inferred from their selecting as a settlement the best position in these seas for commerce, and one of the worst for agriculture. The Malayan town of the 12th century seems to have made as rapid progress under SRI TRIBUANA, as the English one did in the 19th under RAFFLES. The old town speedily became noted as a great emporium, and merchants flocked to it from all quarters. DE BARROS had also heard that " Singapúra was the resort of the navigators of the western seas of " India as well as of those of the eastern seas from Siam, China, Choompa " (Champa), Camboja, and of the many thousand islands which lie towards " the East."

The town must certainly have fallen from any such position at the time when MARCO POLO, the first European who visited the Straits, passed it towards the end of the 13th century. He does not even mention any name like Singapore.

The real history of the Peninsula begins with the foundation of Malacca, which was laid shortly after the fall of Singapore, about 250 years before the arrival of the Portuguese in India. According to the most trustworthy account, it happened as follows :—About that time, one SANGSINGA reigned in Singapore, and in the neighbouring country of Java one PARAVISA, who, at his death, left his sons under the guardianship of his own brother, their uncle : but he having found occasion to murder the eldest, usurped the throne ; at which some of the noble Javanese, being highly disgusted, did, with PARAMISORA, their late King's youngest son, fly to Singapore, where they met with a kind reception from SANGSINGA : but it was not long before PARAMISORA, in combination with his Javanese, murdered SANGSINGA, and put himself in possession of his kingdom. The King of Siam, to avenge the outrage inflicted on SANGSINGA, his vassal and son-in-law, forced the Javanese to quit the country for Moar; and subsequently PARAMISORA transferred his colony to Malacca. The King of Siam's interference was common then. In 1502, only seven years before the Portuguese arrived, he attacked the King of Malacca with a fleet of 200 sails, aboard of which were 6,000 soldiers, under the conduct of the Governor of Ligor; but the fleet was scattered by a storm. In the fifteenth century, a large proportion of the Peninsula, probably all outside the dominions of Johor and Malacca, was, more or less, under the Siamese sovereigns; but since that time, Siam has had its own troubles; and the Peninsula has been mostly divided into the petty States already enumerated, the historical details of which have little interest.

The English began to trade systematically with Malaya in 1602, during Queen ELIZABETH's reign. They had long been preceded by the Portuguese, who settled in Malacca and elsewhere from 1510 to 1640: after which the Dutch in Bantam began to take an aggressive course, and within a few years, all the Portuguese possessions fell into their hands: including Malacca and the kind of sovereignty over the Peninsula which in those days it enjoyed. The Dutch had factories in Pêrak, Pangkor and Kêdah, for the tin trade. These were never long maintained, and gave no political control, and from 1661 to 1818, Pêrak, at any rate, remained independent. In that year it was overrun by the Siamese, but the Penang Government intervened, and the Siamese withdrew in 1821. They have since committed no aggressions on the West coast of the Peninsula South of Province Wellesley, though to the North and East of that Province, their invasions continued till 1832.

Captain LIGHT's occupation and settlement of Penang in 1786 forms the first political connection between the British East India Company and the Malay Peninsula. Penang was completely successful as a trading and shipping station, the population increasing during the first 20 years almost as rapidly as afterwards in Singapore.

The occupation of Malacca in 1795 was undertaken on military grounds, in pursuance of PITT's policy throughout the great war of attacking France through her allies and dependencies.

The foundation of Singapore in 1819 was the natural corollary of the great stroke by which in 1813, "private trade" had been thrown open and monopoly abolished throughout Malaya, during Sir STAMFORD RAFFLES's Government of Java. The new Settlement, of which the immediate and uninterrupted prosperity has born the best testimony to the merits of that bold policy, soon became the capital of the three British possessions in the Peninsula. These were formed into a Colony independent of India in 1867, with the not very happy designation of the "Straits Settlements"

In 1874, the Colony, having already much developed since its transfer from India, was thought by Governor Sir A. CLARKE strong enough to take under its protection and administrative responsibility the Western States of the Peninsula, which were always in trouble: whereas Johor, being already so bound up with Singapore, was in a very different position. These other three littoral States—Pêrak, Sêlângor and Sungei Ujong have,—for the last eight years, and after the brief military occupation of 1876, been in most respects more like an orderly and prosperous portion of the Colony than like the petty and misgoverned Malay States they were before.

Many historical details concerning the Peninsula in the recent times since the advent of Europeans, will be found in the Outline History at the end of this volume.

~~~~~~~~~~~~~~~~~~~~~

CHAPTER III.

NORTHERN (SIAMESE) DIVISION OF THE PENINSULA.

The Siamese, or Thai as they call themselves, have, for some centuries, been connected with the North of the Peninsula: first apparently as settlers, and subsequently, down to quite recent times, as conquerors. Since the decline of the Pegu power, they have claimed the suzerainty over the littoral of the narrow portion of the Peninsula North of 7° of North Latitude, which is approximately the southern limit of their race ; and they exercise a less defined supremacy over Kĕdah on the West, and the Malay States on the East between Sĕnggòra and Pahang (4° North).

The non-Malayan Siamese provinces to the South of the Isthmus of Kra are, successively :—

On the versant of the Bay of Bengal—Renong, Takuapah or Kopah with Takuatung, Panggua, Puket or Junk Ceylon (Ujong Sâlang), and Trang. The island of Junk Ceylon comprises two administrative divisions—that of Talang and that of Tongka.

On the versant of the Gulf of Siam, and extending from North to South, there are the provinces of Chumpon, Langsuan, Chaiya, Bandon, Ligor or Lakhon, and Sĕnggòra. There are also two inland provinces between Trang and Sĕnggòra, almost independent, known as Patĕlûng and Plean.

The chain of mountains which forms the water-parting of the Peninsula divides the littoral States in the interior. These States are under Chinese or Siamese rulers, who are called in Siamese " *Phya*." The population is, in general, Siamese and Chinese, though Ligor has also a large number of Malay inhabitants. The population of all these provinces, together, has been estimated by the latest traveller as high as 500,000 souls. The country is very rich, but extremely little known. A mixed Malayo-Siamese people, commonly known as " Sam-Sam," form a large part of the population in the South of Ligor and Sĕnggòra, and to the North of Kĕdah. Although assimilated to the Siamese in customs, and in religion also as regards Ligor, these Sam-Sam appear to be physically allied to the Malay rather than to the Thai stock.

The following particulars are known of the principal places :—

KRA.—The isthmus of Kra, the North district of lower Siam, connects the Malay Peninsula with Further India, and adjoins the frontier of British Burma. The province extends between latitude 9° and 12° North, with a breadth averaging about 60 miles. Near its centre, on the North Bank of the River Pakshan, is the town of Kra. Coal is recently reported to have been found in its neighbourhood.

RENONG.—One of the principal places on the West coast at the present time is Renong in the North, a tin-producing Settlement, chiefly inhabited by Chinese, and of which, together with Trang, a Penang-born Chinaman is now the feudatory Rāju.

JUNK CEYLON.—Further South is situated the island of Junk Ceylon, or Ujong Sâlang (known to the Siamese as *Puket*), with its two divisions of Talang and Tongka, which lies to the South of the islands of the Mergui Archipelago, in latitude 8° North, longitude 96° East, and occupies a conspicuous position at the North-West elbow of the Peninsula. It is separated from the Continent by Papra Strait ; and is 40 miles in length by 15 in breadth. It formerly belonged to the Râja of Kĕdah, but it has of late years been administered by the Siamese. The principal place is Puket on the sheltered East side of the country, where the Siamese Commissioner usually resides. A large Chinese population is here engaged in tin-mining : the product of which is, for the most part, brought to Penang. On the North of the island is the strait and harbour called Papra, which may be entered at spring tides by ships drawing 20 feet water. From Penang are imported opium and piece-goods, and in return are sent tin, edible birds' nests, beche-de-mer and elephants' teeth. Junk Ceylon enjoys a good climate. The Dutch when paramount at Malacca, in the seventeenth century, had a trading station here.

EAST COAST.

LIGOR (Lĕgor) is called in Siamese *Lakhon*. It is the principal Siamese Province in this part of the isthmus, and was founded four centuries ago by the King of Ayuthia. It has about 150,000 souls, of whom nearly three-fourths are Siamese. Its chief town is Ligor, situated on the northern side of Lakhon Bight, about latitude 8° 17' North and longitude 100° 12' East. The Governor or Chow Phya of Ligor has extensive authority, with the power of capital punishment.

SĔNGGÔRA (*Song Klu*) is the name of the most southerly province of this northern section, and consequently that which borders on the Malayan States of the Peninsula; and it is through the Chinese Governor of Sĕnggôra that the King of Siam has hitherto exercised occasional interference with his Malayan tributaries. Its capital is on the East coast, in the shelter of Tĕntâlam Island. This is a large flat island, lying along the coast, with good pasturage and padi cultivation. Behind is a remarkable deep inland channel, of sweet water, into which the Tĕlûng (Patĕlûng) flows from the Kao Luang (chief mountains).

Inland of this channel lie the small and quasi-independent Sam-Sam States of Patĕlûng and Plean, under a Chinese Râja.

During the North-East monsoon there is little or no communication between the southern provinces of Siam and the capital, as the coast is a complete lee shore.

From Sĕnggôra there is no land passage to Bangkok; but a road was made in the opposite direction, across the Peninsula to Kĕdah, in 1871, at the time of the King of Siam's visit to the Straits.

The administrative provinces and divisions of the Siamese territory in the Malay Peninsula are described, on Siamese authority, as follows :— The Non-Malayan States to the North of Kĕdah are:—

PATĔLŮNG.	CHUMPON.
Plean.	Pratiem.
TAKUAPAH.	Tasa.
Kererat-ne-kom.	Se-wee.
Wakuatuug.	LANOSUAN.
PANGGUA.	RENONG.
PUKET (Junk Ceylon).	KRA.
Talung.	KUMNETNE-PE-KUN.
Tongka.	PRACHUSP-KE-KE-KAN.
CHAIYA.	Pran.
Sompaksou.	
Pa-guan.	

The Malayan States (excluding those under Treaty obligations with the British Government) now tributary to Siam are:—

NAKONSEE-TUMERAT or	*Je-ring.
LAKHON (Ligor).	Rĕmau.
Pĕrlis.	Sai.
Satun (Sĕtûl).	*Rana.
Kanchonedit.	Jalah (Jalo).
Traug.	Nong-chik (Nochi).
SONG-KLA (Sĕnggòra).	Chaua (Chenai).
Tanî (Patâui.)	Tipah.

Further South, on both sides of the Peninsula, lie the tributary Malayan Provinces, with which obligations exist, by Treaty and otherwise, with the British Government, and which are under the practically independent rule of their own Mahomedan Râjas.

KĔDAH.

Kĕdah, called by the Portuguese *Quedah* and by the Siamese *Sai*, is the only Malayan tributary of Siam on the West side. The present State of Kĕdah lies entirely on that coast, between Traug and Pĕrak, from 7° to 5° 30′ North latitude. It is 120 miles in length, and stretches for about 25 to 30 miles inland, so that it is computed to have an area of nearly 4,000 square miles. Besides this territory, a chain of many islands of considerable size, including Lĕngkawi and Trutao, lies along its coasts, and forms part of it, so that its actual area is probably not less than 5,000 square miles. The country is divided

---

* These appear to take the place of the States *Jĕmbu* and *Liyci* in the Malay list of the nine States, given under the heading "Patâni."

23

into three provinces, named after the rivers Sĕtûl to thĕ North, Pĕrlis in the centre, and Kĕdah proper to the South. Kĕdah as a whole is distinguished from the other States of the Peninsula by its comparative freedom from mountain land. The most notable of its mountains is Jĕrei or Kĕdah Peak, over 4,000 feet. It contains at least 26 rivers, 6 of which are of some size, but all of them obstructed at their mouths by bars. In none is there, at spring tides, over 9 feet of water. Between the mainland and the Lĕngkawi islands, there lies an extensive mud bank, so that vessels of any considerable burden cannot come nearer the coast than four miles.

The old town, called "Quedah" by the Portuguese, was situated in latitude 6° North upon one of the larger rivers (it is believed River Merbu) which was navigable for vessels of 300 tons burden.

The geological formation of Kĕdah, generally speaking, is granite, and in places tin is found and, it is believed, gold. But the more important tin mines are just beyond the Kĕdah frontiers; and this holds true both to the North, the East, and the South. Limestone crops out in a remarkable manner at Gûnong Wang, on the river Giti, a tributary of the Muda, and at Gûnong Geriyang, or Elephant Mount. The vegetable products are the usual ones of the Peninsula, the country being particularly well adapted for growing rice. Fruit trees of all kinds, especially the mangostin and durian, grow to great perfection. Among its wild animals, the elephant is common and is used as a beast of burden. Cattle and buffaloes are abundant in the domestic state.

The inhabitants consist of Malays; of a few Sam-Sams or mixed Siamese in the North, who are usually Mahomedan here, and speak both Malay and Siamese; of the Peninsula Negritos; of Mestizo Telingas, speaking both Tamil and Malay; and of a few Chinese. Before the Siamese invasion and conquest of 1821, the country is said to have had a population of over 50,000, which in 1839 was reduced to 21,000. At present, the population must exceed the usual estimate of 30,000 to 50,000 very considerably; the traveller Carl Bock (1884) was told 525,000, the Chinese numbering 24,000, but this is probably excessive. The Malays may safely be put at 100,000; and the Chinese probably exceed 20,000. The whole number is probably within 150,000.

The Capital is Kota Star, or Alor Star, on a river of no great size, though one of the largest of the country, to the North of the conspicuous Mount Jĕrei. It has for some years been connected, by the rough road already mentioned, with Sĕnggôra on the East, the nearest Siamese town of importance. This is at present the only road across the Peninsula. The River Muda, the frontier of Province Wellesley, is navigable for small boats to Baling, distant about 60 miles East. This place is of some importance as the frontier station, near the point where Kĕdah, Pĕrak and Patâni meet; and from Baling the Muda River is used to carry to market at Penang the tin which is found in unusual abundance at Klian Intan and Kroh, on the East or Patâni side of the dividing range of Titi Wangsa.

The country at the back of Province Wellesley is also known to be rich in tin at Serdang and Kûlim, but it has not yet been developed.

It follows from the position of Kĕdah that its trade is almost exclusively with Penang, with which port communication by steamer is now easy and frequent. The exports consist principally of tin, rice, bats' manure (from the lime-stone caves), and jungle produce.

The history of this State, as of all the others of the Peninsula to the North of Malacca, is full of obscurity. Colonel Low discovered in the forests some remains of what he supposed to be Buddhist temples, and some inscriptions in the Pali character, indicating not Malay but Siamese culture. It seems probable that even so late as the beginning of the sixteenth century the Malays here had been but partially converted to Mahomedanism. The earliest authentic information we have of Kĕdah is from the Portuguese writer Barbosa, whose manuscript is dated "Lisbon, 1516;" and he describes it as "a place of the kingdom of Siam," and makes mention of a "Sea-port called Quedah, "to which an infinite number of ships resort, trading in all kinds "of merchandise." Kĕdah, in common with all the other northern States of the Peninsula, has probably been always more or less tributary to Siam, for being, with Patâni, the most northern of all the Malay States, it has been most subject to its direct influence. But the policy of the Siamese Government here, as elsewhere, has been to leave the extraneous races, comprised within the dominion it assumes, to the administration of their own rulers; the Malayan Râja of Kĕdah is thus an hereditary and quasi-independent sovereign. In token of his dependence on Siam he has always sent the King, once in three years, an offering consisting of an artificial flower of gold. Notwithstanding this, the Râja alienated to the Indian Government in 1786 (Captain Light being the Agent) the island of Penang, and subsequently, in 1800, Province Wellesley on the mainland, without reference to Siam, whose alleged suzerainty was neither well understood nor much enforced at that time. By the cession of Penang, Kĕdah lost some of its trade, and though the Râja seems to have acted within his rights, he evidently incurred Siam's displeasure. In 1821, the Siamese from Ligor invaded the country, overran it, and after an occupation of several years, abandoned after ruining it. The prince fled to Penang for protection, and of course received an asylum. His line was restored after many years : but the tendency of the Government at Bangkok to interfere in Kĕdah affairs has since been accentuated, the King of Siam even claiming to nominate as well as confirm the Râja.

PATÂNI.*

In the latitude corresponding to that of Kĕdah on the East coast, the country still commonly known as Patâni is situated between Sĕnggóra and Kĕlantan, 7° to 6° 20′ North, with a coast line on the East side of about 50 miles. Estimated area, 6,000 square miles. The population may be roughly put at 50,000 to 75,000, though Carl Bock (1884) gives

---

* For convenience, *Patâni* is treated of here, though politically it seems to be distinguished from this group, and has been included above in the administrative province of Sĕnggóra.

the number of inhabitants as 200,000, avowedly from Siamese information. The Malays are more numerous, and the Sakei less so, on this than on the other side of the dividing range.

The name "Patàni" is at the present time, except as applied to the River of that name, a merely historical expression, which must be understood to comprise nine small Siamese-Malayan States or divisions. These nine administrative divisions, together with other provinces, are now under the general but ill-defined control of Sénggôra, the seat of Government for the south-eastern coast of the Siamese section of the Peninsula, so far as any administrative suzerainty exists.

Since the country's invasion and subjugation by Siam in 1832, it has been broken up into the four sea-board States or divisions, lying from North to South in the following order:—Nong-chik or Tujong, Patàni, Jèmbu, Sai; and the five interior divisions—Tipah, Chenai, Jalo, Rèman, Ligei. Of these, Rèman is, even excluding any part of the Pêrak watershed, the most extensive, and Patàni with its sea-port, is probably still the most populous. Jalo and Ligei are believed to be the richest in minerals.

The principal physical features of the province are the two considerable rivers—the Patàni and the Télôpin—which rise in the same hills and flow nearly parallel to the sea, through a country for the most part flat, but with isolated cliffs and hills.

The River Patàni is a long but shallow river which retains the same name throughout its whole length. Its source is said to be in the mountain Jambul Mêrak (peacock's crest) about 5° 35', from which also the northern tributaries of the Pêrak flow; thence it has a northerly course and falls into the Gulf of Siam in 6° 55' North. The upper waters of the Rivers Patàni and Pêrak are a labyrinth of streams forming the head-waters of the river system of this part of the Peninsula; the River Kêlantan is also said to take its source in the same region.

The Patàni has an extensive delta, intersected by numerous creeks. Kwâla Tujong to the North is the most important estuary, and is navigable as far as Kwâla Nong-chik (Nochi) where it bifurcates from the Patàni.

The Bay of Patàni is formed by the projection of a narrow strip of land about 7 or 8 miles in length, which, connected with the mainland to the eastward, bends round to the North-west like a horn and protects the roadstead, so that vessels can at most seasons ride in safety; which accounts for the high estimation in which it was held by the early navigators. The western extremity of this projection is called Cape Patàni. The town and port of Patàni is almost all that is left unchanged of the former important State of that name. It was and still is the chief town of the whole of this country. It is situated about 2 miles from the river's mouth, on the South-east side; a fair amount of trade is still carried on with Singapore and Bangkok, as also with the neighbouring Siamese and Malayan States. The exports are tin, lead, gutta, salt-fish, tiles, earthenware and timber. The population of the town consists of Malays, Chinese and Siamese, and is supposed to be from 3,000 to 4,000. The Malay race preponderates, the Rája himself being a Malay. The active commercial and shipping business is controlled by a "Captain China."

RÉMAN.

The largest and perhaps the most important of the provinces at this time is Rêman, lying to the South-east of the river and bordering on Pêrak, with which it is closely connected by ties of intercourse and common interest. It is the most Malayan of all these States; but its Malay Râja is, like the rest, responsible to the Chow Kun, or Governor of Sênggôra, and must look to be confirmed by the King of Siam. Kôta Bharu, some miles on the East side of the Patâni River, is his residence ; and the population of the country is to be found chiefly in this neighbourhood and near the upper valley of the Pêrak, which river the Rêman people use for exporting tin, &c. The boundary with Pêrak, near which are the valuable tin mines of Kroh and Intan, already mentioned in connection with Kêdah, has yet to be determined.

Jalo, situated principally to the North-West of the River Patâni, near the head-waters of the Pêrak, lies under the eastward cliffs of the bold range of Bukit Bêsar. Jalo is believed to be one of the richest mineral countries in the whole Peninsula, having abundant galena, tin, and gold already worked at some points by the Chinese. Like the other mineral countries, it is intersected by remarkable limestone formations.

The galena mines of Patâni, which a few years ago attracted much attention in Singapore, lie near the small town Banisita. This is situated in a picturesque amphitheatre of hills, through which the river flows, about 45 miles distant from the town of Patâni in a straight line, but double that distance by river.

The area of the whole of " Patâni" is about 6,000 square miles, nearly half of which is believed to lie in the two provinces above described.

In 1786, the year of the first Siamese invasion, there were said to be 115,000 inhabitants in the State of Patâni. In 1832, after the second invasion, there were computed to be only 54,000 people in these provinces, and the population has probably not increased since then, except in regard to its Chinese miners, who now number several thousands.

The southernmost of all the nine provinces collectively termed " Patâni " is Sai, beyond which lies the large and important Malayan State called Kêlantan.

KÊLANTAN.

South of Patâni on the East coast lie the Malayan States of Kêlantan and Tringgânu, whose position is one of independence guaranteed by treaty with the British Government, though nominally subject to Siam.

Kêlantan is situated to the South of the Patâni States, the River Banâra being the boundary, between 6° 20' and 5° 40', with about 60 miles of coast on the East side. It has an area of about 7,000 square miles ; with a population of certainly over 100,000 ; but so little is known of the interior that there is no great certainty about either area or population. It is in a prosperous condition, surpassing in population all the Native States on the East coast, and in natural resources and mineral wealth vying with Pahang. It is bounded to the South by Tringgánu, the River Bésút separating them. It has the States of Rëman, Pêrak and Pahang to the West, the eastern ridge of the peninsular chain being considered the boundary. The interior is believed to have a great extent of open country, traversed by the long but shallow River Kêlantan and its tributaries, which, like the River Patâni, flow North. Here there is grown an immense quantity of rice, some of which is exported to Singapore; as also cattle, which are kept in great herds.

The town of Kêlantan is situated near the river's mouth and is a large and flourishing settlement with considerable trade. Its population is said to be over 20,000; and that of the whole State is estimated by the Natives at 600,000, and on good authority as high as 200,000. As far as can be known without a census, it must considerably exceed 100,000. This indicates some recent development of the State; for in 1850, Mr. Crawfurd thought the estimate of 50,000 inhabitants an "exaggeration," though even then the population was called "large."

Its mineral resources comprise tin and gold. Even so far back as 1837 it was stated that 3,000 pikuls of tin were exported annually, and that Kêlantan gold, next to that of Pahang, was the most celebrated among Malays. Lead is also supposed to exist. Much pepper and other articles of export are also cultivated here by the Chinese, and a good deal of jungle produce is collected. The principal trade is with Singapore, and is mainly conducted by the Chinese during the South-West monsoon.

Kêlantan is known to have existed as an integral State at the close of the 15th century and before the arrival of the Portuguese; and in the Malay Annals it is specially stated that during the time of Mahmud II, of Malacca, A. D. 1477, Kêlantan was a kingdom "more powerful than that of Patâni." Like Tringgánu, Kédah and Patâni, it has, from time immemorial, been harassed by the demands of Siam; and, according to the official statement of Mr. Anderson, Political Agent in 1825, repeatedly solicited, in the early days of Penang, the protection of the British Government and the establishment of an English factory, offering very considerable advantages. It has never submitted to Siam further than that, although practically under its own Malay Rája, it has made a customary acknowledgment of dependence by periodically sending to Bangkok a tributary token called "the gold flower."

In 1832, the chief of Patâni, upon the invasion of his country by Siam, fled to Kêlantan, but was delivered up to the Siamese Praklang, who repeatedly ordered the Rája of Kêlantan into his presence. With these mandates the Malay chief did not deem it prudent to comply, but was eventually compelled, it is said, to propitiate his foe, by a large present of specie and gold dust. Newbold pointed out at the time that this was a violation of the 12th Article of Major Bunny's Treaty of 1826, which stipulates that " Siam shall not go and obstruct or interrupt

"commerce in the States of Tringgânu and Kĕlantan. English mer-
"chants and subjects shall have trade and intercourse in future, with
"the same facility and freedom as they have heretofore had; and the
"English shall not go and molest, attack and disturb those States upon
"any pretence whatever." What little trade and intercourse now exist
have passed from the hands of English merchants to those of Chinese
and Native traders.

TRINGGÂNU.

Tringgânu is situated at the widest part of the Peninsula, between
5° 40' and 4° 35' North, and has an area of under 4,000 miles. with a
population of about 20,000. Tringgânu has, for some time past, included
Kĕmâman, which lies along the coast of the Gulf of Siam to the South
of Tringgânu. Its coast line extends along the Gulf of Siam for 80
miles, and is bounded on the South and West by the principality of Pahang, and on the North and North-East by that of Kĕlantan. The River
Bĕsût is its boundary with Kĕlantan, and the River Chĕrûting with Pahang.
To the interior, the high ranges forming the East boundary of
Pahang form a natural frontier, but the boundary is believed to be
otherwise quite undefined. Of its area, nothing certain is known; nearly
the whole country is one continuous jungle, with less development. either of
its minerals or its commerce. than perhaps any other of the Malay States.
The inhabitants consist almost entirely of Malays and some wild tribes,
with a very few Chinese. who carry on the little that is now done in the way
of trade or mining. The total population of the State was computed at
37,500 in 1856. Of this number, the town of Tringgânu, situated in
the northern part of the State, near the mouth of a not very large river,
latitude 5° 25' North, longitude 103° East, was then estimated to contain
from 15,000 to 20,000 inhabitants. or more than half of the population
of the State. A most destructive fire took place in August, 1883, which
is said to have destroyed nearly 2,000 habitations. The town has been
much deserted since, and the population of the whole country has, it is
believed, declined considerably, and does not exceed 20,000 at the
present time, many having been attracted away to Kĕlantan. The
place is but little visited, and the small quantity of gold and tin
produced come, it is said. from the Pahang mountains, which are not so
far removed from the coast at this point. This State is claimed as one of
the hereditary tributaries of Siam, but has always resisted, as far as it
was able to, the assumed supremacy of the Siamese, the population being
almost entirely Mahomedan and Malayan. A "gold flower" is sent periodically to Bangkok. through Sĕnggôra, in token of its nominal dependence.

Kĕmâman (River and District) was, according to Malay tradition, formerly a province of Pahang. and, on this ground, still considers itself free
from even nominal allegiance to Siam. This recognition is, however, admitted by Tringgânu, with which country Kĕmâman seems to be now politically incorporated. It is a place of no importance, lying midway between

Pahang and Tringgânu. The town is only a mile or two from the mouth of the river of the same name, in lat. 4° 15' North. It is a settlement of modern origin, and probably owes its existence to the tin-mines, discovered early in the century in the neighbourhood. The district is scarcely 1,000 square miles in area : and is, or until recently was, under the direct control of a separate chief, under Tringgânu. Its population was estimated in 1839 at 1,000 Malays and Chinese. It produces tin, a little gold, camphor, ebony, &c. According to a Mr. Medhurst, who visited the place in 1828, Kĕmâman at first yielded a considerable revenue to the Sultan of Tringgânu, but afterwards the mines failed, and the Chinese dispersed. It is believed to be scarcely more prosperous at the present time than it was in 1839.

Between the Rivers Kĕmâman and Tringgânu lie the smaller districts of Paka, Dúngún and Marang, which, like Kĕmâman, are each under a chief, subordinate to Tringgânu.

CHAPTER IV.

SOUTHERN (BRITISH) DIVISION OF THE PENINSULA.

THE British Section of the Peninsula, as distinguished from the northern portion under Siamese influence, is merely a political division, and has nothing to do with any physical or other natural boundary. The two sections have never been delimited, and in the interior no precise boundaries can possibly exist. The line is approximately as given on page 6, and runs with the southern boundaries, whatever they may be, of Kĕdah, Rĕman and Tringgânu. The northern limits of the Malay race, however, lie considerably to. the North of any such line ; and the administrative interference of Siam is throughout very slight, and, as mentioned in the last

Chapter, is scarcely permitted at all among the Malayan States.

A few words regarding the Malay race, its history and its language, will be in place here, this Southern Division being essentially the *Malay* Peninsula.

It is difficult to understand how it happened that a great race like the Malays—colonisers by instinct, and whose history and traditions show no little aptitude for organisation—should, in the last century, have degenerated into the pirates and general enemies of commerce, with which the Malay name is, or was till late years, almost synonymous.

Sir HOME POPHAM, who was acquainted with the people in the early days of Penang when we first settled in the Straits, throws some light on their disorganised state. He says (1798) that " previous to the establishment of Dutch power, and the " prevalence of Dutch avarice, the Malayans were as indus- " trious and ingenious as the other inhabitants of the country ; " with that superiority of activity and enterprise over more " inland inhabitants, which a maritime situation invites and " produces. While the English continued to possess a con- " siderable share of the trade of those countries, the Malayan " character remained unimpaired ; but after the declension of " our interest in that part of India, when the Dutch became " paramount, their tyranny first repressed the exertion of " Malayan ability, and, afterwards, according to the usual " progressive effects of slavery, reduced them to ignorance. " Still, however, they retain some vestiges of their original " character, and show that a different treatment and example " may work a complete change ; as some of them, from their " intercourse with the English, are fast improving in activity

" and industry, of which they are themselves allowed to reap
" the fruits."

It may now be said that these hopes have been realised,
during the past century, both in the Peninsula and Borneo.
During this period, there has also been shown among the
whole Malayan stock an unexpected vigour and vitality.
The populations of Java and Sumatra, and of the Malayan
portions of the Peninsula, far from showing any tendency to
dwindle away before the increasing Europeans and Chinese,
have multiplied prodigiously; and are, taken all together, certainly three or four times as great as at the beginning of the
century. In our own Colony, the numbers of the Malays
alone have grown from under 30,000 in Penang and Malacca
at that time, to nearly six times the number at the last
census.

The wide dispersion of the Malay language has always been
remarkable. Wherever one goes—for more than 2,000 miles,
from Achin to New Guinea, and amid an endless variety of
races—is found the convenience of a common speech. Something is due to the language itself, but much to the maritime
instincts of the people, which have spread its use.

And this brings up the long-discussed question of their
origin, which has a special interest in treating of the Malay
Peninsula.

The true centre of dispersion of the Malay race may be
fixed rather in Malacca than in Sumatra, contrary to the
generally received opinion. If the Malays are physically allied
to the Mongol stock, it is obvious that the earliest migration
must have been from High Asia towards the Peninsula, and
thence to Sumatra, possibly at a time when the island still

formed part of the mainland. The national traditions of a dispersion from Měnangkâbau or Palembang, in South Sumatra, must, accordingly, be understood to refer to later movements, and more especially to the diffusion of the civilised Malay peoples, who first acquired a really national development in Sumatra in comparatively recent times. VALENTYN long ago pointed out that the name is specially applied in Sumatra to the great Sungei-pâgû-Malâyu tribe, of the Sungei-pâgû auriferous district, and it seems, on the whole, most probable that it was originally the name of some local tribe there, which rose to pre-eminence.

From this point, they spread to the Peninsula, to Borneo, Sulu, and other parts of Malaya, apparently after their conversion to Islam, although there is reason to believe that other waves of migration must have reached Further India, and especially Camboja, if not from the same region, at all events from Java, at much earlier dates. The impulse to these earlier movements must be attributed to the introduction of Indian culture through the Hindu and Buddhist missionaries, perhaps two or three centuries before the Christian era. During still more remote prehistoric times, various sections of the Malay and Indonesian stocks were diffused westwards to Madagascar, where the Hovas, of undoubted Malay descent, still hold the political supremacy ; and eastwards to the Philippines, Formosa, and the interior of Hainan. This astonishing expansion of the Malayan people throughout the Oceanic area is sufficiently attested by the diffusion of a common Malayo-Polynesian speech from Madagascar to Eastern Island, and from Hawaii to New Zealand.

These are the views now generally accepted. They were

propounded originally by the well-known J. R. LOGAN, and are
now adopted authoritatively by the *Encyclopedia Britannica*,
1883. A tabular arrangement will best define the exact position
of our Malays. A classification of the various branches and
sub-branches of this Malayan stock has, therefore, been extracted from the same authoritative source ; which gives, in a
brief summary, the results of the vast deal of controversy and
scholarship expended on the subject in recent years. It
must be understood, to begin with, that in the general scheme
of inter-oceanic races, the Malayan stock itself is considered
by ethnologists to be but one of four main stocks, the others
being the Papuan, the Mahori, and the Mikronesian. The
component parts of the main Malayan stock are as follows :—

Órang Maláyu:—Měnangkábau, Palembang, and Lampong
in Sumatra ; the States of the Malay Peninsula ; Borneo ;
Ternate.

Sumatran group :—Achinese, Rejangs, Passumahs.

Javanese group :—Javanese proper, Sundanese, Madurese,
Balinese.

Celebes group :—Bugis, Mang Kassara, and others.

Philippine group:—Tagalas, Bisayans, Bicol, Sulu, and others.

Outlying groups :—Hovas of Madagascar, Formosan islanders.

In all these, the distinctly Malay physical type decidedly
predominates; whereas elsewhere in the Archipelago, the so-
called Malays are often rather " Indonesians," in whom the
distinctly Caucasic physical type predominates. Such especially are the Battaks and Órang Kubu of Sumatra, the
Nias and Mentawey islanders, the Kayans, and many of the
Dyak tribes of Borneo.

The Malayan inhabitants of the southern section of the Peninsula all belong to the first division (the *Órang Maláyu* proper) in the above classification, with the exception of a few Javanese and Bugis in the towns, and a small but increasing number of Sumatrans in the country districts.

The whole number of the Malays in the Peninsula, though they certainly stand first among our numerous races, is probably not much more than half of the entire population of this southern section with which we are now dealing, or nearly 400,000 in all, the Chinese race coming second in number. Apart from the Colony, this section of the Peninsula itself is most thinly inhabited, having only about 300,000 souls, even more so than the northern section, which has been described in Chapter II as containing 400,000, and which there is now reason to think is much under-estimated, the number of inhabitants being, in fact, not less than 700,000.

Politically, this Section is divided into :—

1.—The Protected States of Pêrak, Sĕlángor, and Sungei Ujong, occupying the West coast, from Kĕdah to Malacca.

2.—The small inland States behind Malacca called the " Nĕgri Sĕmbĭlan."

3.—Pahang, on the East coast.

4.—Johor, comprising the whole southern extremity.

5.—The Colony of the Straits Settlements.

Each of these sub-divisions is treated of separately in the following descriptions.

PROTECTED STATES.

The Protected Native States make the British administration of the West Coast complete from Penang to Malacca, and comprise Pêrak, Sĕlângor, and Sungei Ujong. Their order of importance is in accordance with the order in which they stand.

PÊRAK.

The State of Pêrak lies next to Kĕdah and Province Wellesley, on the West coast of the Peninsula. The State is situated between the parallels of 5° 10′ and 3° 45′ North latitude, and 100° 22′ to 102° East longitude; the greatest length being in a North and South direction, and amounting to nearly 100 miles; the breadth from the coast to the East is still uncertain, but is probably somewhat less.

Pêrak is bounded on the North by Province Wellesley (Trans-Krian district) from Sungei Bakau on the coast to Parit Buntar. From that point the boundary runs to the source of the Krian River, in the Gûnong Inas range, the boundary between Kĕdah and Pêrak being the Krian River. The most northerly point at which Kĕdah and Pêrak touch is popularly said to be a swamp or lake, called Tasek, some miles East of Baling. Between this point and the source of the Krian, the range of mountains which forms the water-shed of the Pêrak river is the western boundary of Pêrak. From Tasek eastward, Pêrak is bounded on the North and East by the " Patâni " States of Jalo and Rĕman, but the exact course of the boundary line is undetermined, and is at present the subject of negotiations with Siam.

From Sungei Bakau to Sungei Bĕrnam,* Pêrak is bounded by the sea. On the East, the line of the inner range of mountains, which is the water-shed of the Plus, Kinta and Kampar, Bâtang Padaug and Bidor, with the other tributaries of the Pêrak river, forms the eastern boundary of Pêrak as far as the sources of the river Slim. On the South, Pêrak is bounded by the river Bĕrnam.

For commercial purposes, the State of Pêrak has the advantage of lying only a short distance to the South-East of Penang, which is at present its chief port of shipment, and with which daily steam communication is maintained.

Extent, &c.—The area of the State, including the whole of the Pêrak valley, approaches 8,000 square miles. Mr. DEANE, who was employed on a survey in 1879, estimated it to be approximately 7,900 statute miles (exclusive of the disputed area beyond Bukit Naksa). Of this, he computed that about 2,000 square miles were occupied by hills from 1,500 to 8,000 feet high.

The surface is thus almost equally divided between hill and plain. The principal mountains are the Titi Wangsa and Gûnong Hijau (Lârut) chains, Gûnong Bûbû, and the inland ranges of which Gûnong Bĕsar, Mount Robinson, and Mount Tĕngah (or Tangga) are respectively the central peaks. In these mountains rise the River Plus, the Kinta and the Kampar, the Bidor and the Songkei, the Slim, and the Sĕmbĭlan (a feeder of the Pahang).

The mountain ranges are generally of granitic formation, but, in strong contrast to their usually round surfaces, the sharp peaks and crags of limestone formation crop up here and there throughout the country. The principal of these are Gûnong Kĕndrong, Gûnong Kernei, and Bukit Kâjang in the North; Bâtu Kurau and Gûnong Pondok: some un-named hills in the Plus ranges, and numerous peaks almost throughout the Kinta valley.

The caves in the limestone mountains furnish bats' guano—an excellent manure. This, as well as lime, is available for both mountain and low country cultivation.

The Residency.—The seat of the Government of the British Resident is a small village called *Kwâla Kangsar*. It is situated on the upper waters of the Pêrak, about 23 miles from the present port of Têluk Kêrtang, on the Lârut River, with which it is connected by a good road. It lies about 100 miles up the Pêrak river, and, therefore, the Lârut road gives the most direct access to Penang.

The country can best be described as consisting physically of three principal water-systems—that of the Krian to the North, that of the Pêrak in the centre, and that of the Bêrnam to the South. Each will be described in turn. But the tin-mining district of Lârut, which belongs to neither of these physical divisions, has played and still plays so important a part in the development of the State, that it deserves first mention.

Lârut.

Lârut is situated about midway between the River Krian and the River Pêrak, not more than 10 miles from the sea.

For about thirty years, Chinese miners have worked the extensive tin deposits of great richness at the base of the high mountain range called Gûnong Hijau, and on each side of a small river called Sungei Lârut. This place was found by the early pioneers to be not only rich in tin, but most advantageously situated in respect of commercial intercourse with the British port of Penang, some sixty miles distant. It is seldom that the tin-deposits are found so near the sea. Lârut is under the immediate charge of an Assistant Resident.

Thaipeng, the principal town, now contains 35,000 people, including the adjacent mines. It may thus be reckoned the largest town on the West coast, Malacca not excepted. It is the centre of the mining industry, and is about eight miles from the sea-coast. It is the head-quarters of the chief departments of the State. Thaipeng is connected with Kwâla Kangsar by a carriage-road, and by a line of telegraph. The main road to the sea has hitherto been from Thaipeng to Têluk Kêrtang, but a short line of railway, intended to connect Thaipeng with Port Weld (8 miles), is now completed, as well as a line of road from Lârut to the Krian River, which will open up communication by land with Province Wellesley. There is also telegraph communication with Penang.

The three river systems which, as it has been said, mark the natural divisions of the State, have now to be described in turn, proceeding from the North.

KRIAN.

Krian is an agricultural district adjoining Province Wellesley, the seat of extensive sugar and rice cultivation. This district has a large Malay population, consisting principally of settlers from Penang, Province Wellesley and Kedah. A good many Chinese and Tamil planters have recently settled there.

Sĕlâma, 70 miles up the Krian river, on a large tributary of that name, forms a tin-mining settlement, which a few years ago was more flourishing than at present. It is situated near the principal bifurcation of the Krian. There is a colony of Sumatran Malays at Sĕlâma, and some Chinese miners.

PÉRAK.

The Pérak may be considered the largest and certainly the most important rivers on the West of the Peninsula. It drains not only the extensive valley of the State to which it gives its name, but also receives the drainage of the considerable Kinta district, comprising together at least half the area of the State. It is navigable for steamers as far as Tĕluk Anson, the capital of Lower Pérak. Its source is said to be in the frontier mountain Jambul Mérak, from which the Tĕlôpin and Patâni also take their rise. Its whole length is about 250 miles. At first it flows down in a south-westerly direction towards the sea, receiving, from the West, the Rui, the Kĕndrong, and the Kĕnĕring; and from the East, the Sengro and the Tĕmangau. From Kwâla Kĕnĕring its course is due South. All its main affluents from this point flow into it from the East, viz., the Plus, the Kinta, the Bâtang Padang, and near its estuary the small river Sungei Jandarâta, which almost connects the streams of the Pérak and Bérnam rivers, here flowing parallel at no great distance from each other. The Pérak empties itself into the straits, a few miles to the South of the Dindings. It has a wide estuary, but here, as in other rivers in the Peninsula, shallow water on the bar at the mouth impedes navigation. The principal places on this river are :—Kôta Stia, Tĕluk Anson, Durian Sabâtang, Bandar, Kôta Lumut, Bandar Bhâru (the former Residency near the junction of the Kinta), Pulau Tiga, Lamboh. Bota, Blanja, *Kwâla Kangsar* (the present Residency), Sayong (the residence of H. H. the Regent), Kôta Lama, Chigar Galak, and Kôta Tampan.

Tin is found almost throughout the valley, but in greatest quantity near the East bank of the Pérak and in the Kinta district. The Kinta district includes the territory watered by the river of that name and its tributaries. A Collector and Magistrate has charge of it, and resides at Bâtu Gâjah on the Kinta river. Other places of importance in the district are Lahat, Papan, Ipoh, Pĕngkâlen Pĕgû, Kôta Bhâru, Pĕngkâlen

Bháru (Sungei Raya), Gópeng (a large Chinese mining settlement), Kampar, and Chĕndĕriang.

BĔRNAM.

The southernmost district of the State is that of the river Bĕrnam, probably the largest river, in regard to volume of water, to be found in the Peninsula. It is about two miles wide at the mouth, and navigable for large steamers for many miles. Though draining a very different district, its mouth is less than twenty miles from that of the Pĕrak.

Proceeding up the Bĕrnam, almost due East, the chief places (though none of them are of any size) are *Sabah*, about 20 miles from the mouth ; *Tĕluk Kwali*, about 73 miles from the sea, where the river is still about 120 yards wide and very deep ; *Changkat Bĕrtam*, 85 miles by river from the sea, a small rising ground planted with durian trees, and occupied by a colony of a few Malays. Above this spot stretches an immense expanse of unhealthy swampy country for miles on both sides of the river : through this swamp the river Bĕrnam winds down from *Godangsa*, 111 miles by river from the sea, where the land again becomes higher. A series of canals or cuttings, shortening the navigation of the river, and making it available for steam-launches, have recently been made from this point, through the Changkat Bĕrtam swamp. The distance for boats is, it is computed, thus reduced from 111 miles to about 50 miles.

KWÁLA SLIM, about 130 miles up the river, is the principal station and the Collectorate of the district. It is situated at the bifurcation of the main stream : above this the river divides into two branches of similar size—the river Slim running down from the direction of Pĕrak in the North-East, and the river Bĕrnam from Sĕlángor in the South-East. A hilly region called Changkat Lĕla divides these branches.

ULU SLIM lies about 30 miles higher, at the confluence of the river Slim and the river Gĕliting. It is described as very picturesque—" it might almost be in Switzerland." From here there is an overland path to the Pĕrak waters (river Songkei) of no great distance : and it is known that some of the affluents of the Pahang river flowing into the Gulf of Siam have their source in the same mountains. In the Pĕrak-Pahang boundary rises this Slim branch. The water-shed of the other great branch (the River Bĕrnam) which flows from the South, is in a similar manner to be found at the Sĕlángor-Pahang boundary. At Ulu Slim, land has been successfully opened up by English coffee planters within the last few years.

The highest station on the Bĕrnam river is Tanjong Malim, a fertile, well-cultivated station at the foot of the dividing range. The main road to Sĕlángor and Bĕrnam passes through Tanjong Malim.

General Aspects.

Inhabitants.—At Lárut, and at the chief mining settlements in the interior—in the valleys of the Kinta, Bátang Padang, &c.—the Chinese form the bulk of the population, and were recently estimated as follows :—

Lárut,	... ...	... 35,000
Kinta,	... ...	... 4,000
Lower Pêrak, including Bâtang Padaug and Bidor,	...	... 2,000
Krîan and Kurau,	..	... 5,000
Kwâla Kangsar and Salak,		... 1,000
Sêlâma,	... ...	1,000
	Total,	48,000

The Malay population of the State probably numbers at least 50,000. *Products.*—The chief export is tin, amounting, in 1883, to $2,000,000 ; and the abundance of this metal is the most important economic feature of the State at present. The other exports amount to $3,500,000 (including sugar $307,236) ; and the whole trade, imports and exports, is now (1883) of the value of $10,500,000. There is now daily communication by trading steamers between Penang and Lárut. A steamer also touches at Durian Sabâtang on her fortnightly voyages between Singapore and Penang, and there is a separate service between Penang and Têluk Anson. There is also regular steam communication between Penang and Bêrnam. *Government.*—The government is carried on under the Râja Muda, as Regent, aided and advised by a British Resident, and a Council consisting of the Resident and Assistant Resident, and Native Chiefs of rank and influence.

The Revenue and Expenditure (1883) were as follows :—

Revenue,	...	... $1,474,330
Expenditure,	...	... 1,231,900

and they contrast very remarkably with those of the first year of protection in 1876—Revenue, $213,412 (Lárut only) : Expenditure, $226,379.

A military police force of 700 men, mainly Sikhs, is maintained to secure order, with half a battery of Artillery.

The Collectorates are at *Lárut* : at *Parit Buntar* and *Sêlâma* (for Krîan) : *Kwâla Kangsar*, the seat of the Residency : *Têluk Anson* (for Pêrak river) : *Bâtu Gâjah* (for Kinta district) ; *Kwâla Slim* (for the Bêrnam).

History.—The State of Pêrak is among the older States of the Peninsula, and its history was maintained with scarcely a break for at least 300 years. It was, in the days of the Portuguese, and until the close of the 17th century, subject to Achin, but otherwise it appears to have maintained its independence throughout. It was overrun in the course of the Siamese troubles in 1821 by Kêdah. The Dutch tried, with varying success, to maintain a trading monopoly of the tin for 150 years, but their attempts to obtain a footing were not successful ; though it seems that when they surrendered Malacca in 1795, a small garrison was still kept up there.

All European interference with Pêrak then ceased until 1818 ; when, in consequence of the cession of Malacca to the Dutch, the Penang Government entered into commercial treaties with Pérak, among other Native States, to forestall any fresh attempts at Dutch monopoly. This alliance proved useful to Pérak a few years later, when the Siamese attempted to overrun the country, but were checked from Penang.

The recent development of events dates from the rise of Lârut into importance under No. 1 Jafar, in 1852, consequent upon the discovery of the rich tin deposits there. The Chinese then came in great numbers, and before long the Malay Government naturally fell to pieces. After some years of anarchy, Governor Sir Andrew Clarke interfered in January, 1874, and the Pangkor Treaty was made, introducing the "Protected States" experiment. The small rising that brought upon Pérak a military occupation, after the assassination of the first Resident, Mr. Birch, (1875) led to the adoption of the more robust policy under which Pérak has made its subsequent rapid advances. The State is now about to open the first railway in the Peninsula, or anywhere in Asia to the South of Rangoon.

SÈLÁNGOR.

The Protected State of Sèlángor adjoins Pérak along its whole southern frontier. It is situated between the parallels of 3° 45' and 2° 40' North, with a rather greater extent of coast-line on the East shore of the straits than its northern neighbour Pérak. Area between 4,000 and 5,000 square miles. Population about 50,000.

Sèlángor is a comparatively recent State, the western part of its territory having apparently been left unoccupied from time out of mind, to a greater degree than any other portion of the Peninsula. The southern division was formerly a separate State—Klang (Kèlang)—one of the four original States of the "Negri Sembilan" confederation.

Under the name of Sèlángor are included four main districts, each having a considerable river, named respectively Bérnam, Sèlángor, Klang, and Langat; Bérnam to the North, and the others further South in the order in which they are named. With the exception of Klang and the mouth of the River Sèlángor, the whole territory of the State was absolutely terra incognita until quite lately. Lûkût, now comprised in the Sungei Ujong frontiers, was formerly part of Sèlángor. Being rich in tin found close to the shore, and being situated at a distance of only 40 miles from Malacca, this district was, under a former Râja, the most thriving in Sèlángor.

The greater part of Sèlángor is an extremely level country, stretching inland about 30 miles in the South, and nearly 50 miles in the North, and as yet but little cleared and very thinly inhabited. In its wide versant it presents a marked contrast to Pérak, and especially because its rivers flow almost due West instead of southward. In the interior are some high spurs thrown out from the great mountain chain, especially between Ulu Sèlángor and Ulu Langat, and in the neighbourhood of Kwála Lumpor, the present capital. These spurs have an altitude of about 2,000 feet, with numerous high peaks, where they join the chain, reaching to more than 5,000 feet. The highest is Bukit Těngah, of 6,200 feet, in the Gûnong Kali spur.

At Ginting Bidei, 22 miles North-East of Kwâla Lumpor, there is a pass into Pahang at the junction of two important spurs, one running due South behind Kwâla Lumpor, the source of the river Klang; the other trending away inland, leaving a valley which widens to about 10 or 12 miles, down which flows the Ulu Langat. Several of the highest peaks in this group rise to above 5,000 feet.

Further North, the river Sělângor rises among even higher summits in the central chain, which is here at its nearest point to the river Pahang, of which the tributaries flow down to the East from the same hills. The highest peaks after Bukit Těngah are :—Gûnong Râja, 5,450 feet; Gûnong Chimběras, 5,050 feet; Gûnong Péchěras, 5,650 feet; and Bukit Kanching. from which rises Sungei Bûlû (South of Sělângor) and which is one of the few hills thrown forward into the plain.

Boundaries.—Sělângor is separated from Pêrak by the Bērnam river, which forms its northern boundary. Its extent along the coast is about 100 miles, as far as the river Nîpah to the South (since the 1877 boundary was fixed), and then by a line running to the North and East as far as the hills which divide it from Jělěbu.

In Sělângor, the following are the principal places, all of the size of villages rather than towns, though the new capital and Residency town i growing fast :—

Kwâla Lumpor is, and has been for many years, the centre of the tin-mining of the country. In 1879 it was made the capital, instead of Klang. Its distance from the nearest navigable waters (24 miles) is its principal drawback ; but it is well placed for inland communications, and a railway is to be constructed to connect it with Klang.

Klang.

Klang, the principal port of the country, 12 miles up the river, was the former seat of Government and the first Residency. It is situated near the sea, and many miles from the vicinity of the tin-mines at the foot of the mountains, but is favoured with a navigable river which, owing perhaps to the island Kalang lying across its mouth, is without the almost invariable bar.

Sělângor.

Sělângor, lying at the mouth of the river Sělângor. The river is shallow and practicable only for vessels of small burden. The Dutch had formerly an establishment at Sělângor for the monopoly of the tin ; and a stone fort of their construction is still a conspicuous object, having formerly been, next to Malacca, the most important construction of the kind in these waters.

Langat.

The other towns of Sělângor are *Langat, Bandar Kanching, Jugra* (where the Sultan resides), and *Ulu Langat* and district. This latter lies more inland than any other part of the State.

A good bridle road is now (1884) almost completed from Berânang to Ulu Bêrnam, connecting Sungei Ujong with Pêrak by means of a main road through the whole length of Sëlângor from South to North.

Population.—The population is scanty : no enumeration has yet been taken, but it is supposed not to exceed 50,000, **of** whom more than 30,000 are Chinese. The native inhabitants are believed to be the descendants of a colony of Bugis, from Goa, in the Celebes, who settled here and at Kwâla Linggi under their Chief, Anon Passarai, towards the commencement of the last century. The population about ten years ago had fallen away to a minimum, in consequence of the incessant quarrels and misrule of its princes. It has been much increased of late years, both by Chinese settlers and miners, and by the immigration of Malays from less prosperous States in its neighbourhood, including not a few from Sumatra.

Products.—Sëlângor produces tin of excellent quality, and the deposits at Ulu Langat and Kwâla Lumpor have proved extremely rich, the latter's output (under the name of Klang tin) having attracted much attention for the last twenty years. For some years past, it has stood second only to that of Lârut. Besides tin, there is little else but jungle produce, though important plantations of coffee, pepper, sugar, &c., have been commenced. Tin exports, 1883, reached nearly $2,000,000. The revenue for 1883 amounted to $450,644.

Government.—An incessant quarrel, chiefly as to the rights over the tin duties levied in Klang and Sëlângor, prevailed from 1867 to 1873. At the time when Governor Sir Andrew Clarke was settling the affairs of the Native States in 1874, he undertook to assist the Government of Sëlângor. The Government of this State has since been carried on under the same system as Pêrak.

It has been stated that a railway is in contemplation from Kwâla Lumpor to Klang, and it is certain that roads will shortly connect Sëlângor with Pêrak, as it is already connected with Sungei Ujong and Malacca. It may confidently be hoped that a country with such mineral resources, and such fine hills and plains, drained by abundant rivers like the Bêrnam, Klang, Sëlângor, and Langat, will, under a peaceful rule, become populous and wealthy.

SUNGEI UJONG.

The smallest of the three Protected States is that of Sungei Ujong, to the South of Sëlângor, which lies inland, between that State, Jëlëbu and Rëmbau, to the North-West of Malacca. It was one of the four original States out of which grew the " Nëgri Sëmbîlan."

Extent, &c.—The area of Sungei Ujong is, including the districts of Lûkut and Sungei Râya, about 500 square miles ; the circle of hills to the northward attains an altitude of between 3,000 and 4,000 feet; the State lies mainly on the North bank of the river Linggi. Sungei Ujong suffered for many years from the Selångor disturbances, and others of its own, which owed their origin to the same cause—to quarrels over the tin-royalties. But Sungei Ujong has always been, especially since the development of its mines, the leading State of the Negri Sembilan.

The Linggi River, its one large stream (the highway to Sungei Ujong and much of Rémbau) had, in 1873, been rendered impassable by constant border fights between these two States. After repeated complaints on the part of British subjects in Malacca of the violence and extortion that put a stop to all traffic on the River Linggi, Sir ANDREW CLARKE, Governor in 1874, went personally to Sempang on the Linggi River, and re-opened trade and suppressed disturbance. A Residency was established in Sungei Ujong shortly after, to prevent further disturbance, and to protect the large number of Chinese miners working there.

The mountains of Sungei Ujong approach the sea more nearly than those of Selångor, the interval being, however, even more uncleared and swampy than in the northern State. In former times, Sungei Ujong seems to have been a wholly inland State, but since Residents have been stationed in Selångor and Sungei Ujong, the frontier line between them has been modified : and now the river Lûkut and district, formerly renowned for its tin, but since 1860 almost deserted, are included in Sungei Ujong, thus giving it 20 miles of coast, between Sungei Nîpah and Kwâla Linggi.

The tin workings, and the most inhabited portion of this small State, lie in a sort of semicircular valley, between the hills Brimbûn (4,000 feet), in which the Linggi rises, and Tangga (1,800 feet), the Jélébu boundary, and Perhintian Rimpun (2,000 feet), at the Selångor boundary.. Mount Brimbûn is, in some respects, the key to this State, and, it may be said, to the whole of this part of the country. On the South side of this mountain flows the Moar, and on the East a feeder of the Pahang—River Triang.

Through a gap called Bukit Pûtus, between this mountain and Gûnong Angsi, to the South, is a pass leading to Sri Mènanti and the other Negri Sembilan States.

Population, Products, &c.—The Malay population is almost entirely agricultural, and is mostly found near the mountains, as at Pantei. The whole population is probably below 14,000 souls. Sungei Ujong has abundance of water, and its land is considered suitable for the cultivation of coffee, cocoa, cinchona, &c., which are being grown both on the hills and plains. On the lower ground, tapioca is now largely cultivated. Tin mining is still carried on to a considerable extent by the Chinese at Ampangan, near the Residency, and its neighbourhood. These Chinese miners in Sungei Ujong, as in Lârut, have been the real sinews and wealth-producing power of the country.

A road now connects Sèremban with Pèngkålan Kompas, the newly-opened port near the mouth of the Linggi, and there is regular communication by steam-launch between Malacca and the Linggi. Not far above Pĕngkâlan Kompas are Permâtang Pâsir, the former inconvenient "port," and Linggi village. The Residency is at Sĕremban, about 22 miles higher up the country. Two miles nearer the port is Râsa, the Customs' station at the bridge over the Linggi River; to which the stream is, or was before this new road was made, navigable and clear for small boats. From Sĕremban, roads have been made to Pantei (8 miles), and will, in another year, be completed, so as to connect Sĕlângor on the one side, and Malacca on the other : and with this first instalment of the future road up the Peninsula, Sĕremban, and Sungei Ujong generally, have a fine central position.

Government, &c.—The residential system was introduced here shortly after its adoption in Pêrak and Sĕlângor (December, 1874), and with a short break, at the time of the Pêrak war, that form of government has since been peacefully carried on in the manner already described.

Revenue for 1883, . .	. $117,145
Expenditure for 1883,	153,686.

THE NĔGRI SĔMBĬLAN STATES.

These small States, formerly a kind of confederacy of Nine States, of which the name alone now survives, occupy about 2,000 square miles of the interior of the Peninsula, between the Protected States on the North, Malacca on the West, Johor on the South, and Pahang on the East.

Apart from Klang (which has long formed part of Sĕlângor), Sungei Ujong (which, as a Protected State, is now on a different footing), and Sĕgâmat and Nâning (which have more recently been incorporated with Moar and Malacca, respectively), the Nĕgri Sĕmbĭlan contain a total population of not more than 30,000, mostly to be found in Rĕmbau and Sri Mĕnanti.

Originally there appear to have been four States, which were afterwards broken up and modified as shown below :—

Formerly.	At present.
Klang	—
Sungei Ujong.	—
Jĕlĕbu.	Jĕlĕbu.
Johol.	Johol.
	Inas *or* Jĕlei.
	Ulu Moar *or* Sri Mĕnanti.
	Jĕmpol.
	Rĕmbau.
(Four States.)	(Six States.)

Of these six States, those of sufficient importance to deserve special description are Jĕlĕbu, Johol, Sri Mĕnanti and Rĕmbau.

Before entering upon details, one common feature of interest should be mentioned. These States have apparently originated in the

organisation of the aboriginal tribes, always numerous in this part of the
Peninsula. A large foreign element has since been introduced, especially
from Sumatra. In the days when Johor was powerful, the Něgri Sěmbî-
lan were under the Sultan of Johor : but about 1773. Johor being indifferent about the government of these remote tribal States, allowed the Dutch
to obtain for them, at their request, a Prince of true Měnangkâbau descent,
who, as Yang-di-Pertûan Běsar, ruled over the Confederacy. The States
were thus formally federated, each separate State retaining, however, its
own Pěnghûlu or Dato'. The real power in these States is vested in the
Pěnghûlu, that of the suzerain being nominal only.

This Sumatran immigration, and the political intercourse of the independent Princes of Sumatra with those of the Peninsula, deservedly attracted the attention of scholars like MARSDEN, LEYDEN and RAFFLES ;
but the whole arrangement was of too artificial a kind to last long,
and after five accessions of Měnangkâbau Princes, they ceased to be
invited over there (1820). It is noteworthy, however, that even the
more civilised Malays, especially in Rěmbau, still hold to the tribal
organisation: the very names of many of their tribes, such as "Anak
Acheh " (children of Achin) and " Sri Lěmak Měnangkâbau," betraying
their comparatively recent migration from Sumatra.

JÉLÉBU.

Jélébu is a small State lying to the North and East of Sungei Ujong
and containing about 400 square miles, and under 1,000 inhabitants. It
belongs *politically* to the West coast, though *physically* to the East coast. It
has thus a peculiarly central position in regard to this region of the Peninsula, being situated at the great water-parting ôf the southern portion of it.
Jélébu has, until the present year, remained unexplored. It lies between
Sungei Ujong and the valley of the River Pahang, having Sělângor to the
North and Jěmpol to the South. The country is a succession of narrow
valleys between hills of no great height, except in the South where they
culminate towards Gûnong Brimbûn. These hills are the sources of many
of the principal rivers on both sides of the Peninsula—the Linggi and the
Moar flowing to the West, and the Serting and Triang to the East, both these
being feeders of the Pahang. Comprising as it does the Triang valley,
Jélébu's boundaries are necessarily defined by hills alone, except towards
Pahang. Gěnting Pireh is the boundary towards Sělângor. It is about
28 miles from Ulu Langat, and not far from the mining settlement at
Sungei Lui. Bukit Tangga (1,800 feet), at the head of the Klawang valley, lies between Jélébu and Sungei Ujong, and deserves notice as the
furthest western point of the East coast watershed. Jâwi-Jâwi Bětâub,
on the Triang, is claimed by Jélébu as the eastern boundary towards Pahang, but this has still to be settled. Meanwhile Sungei Dua has been
adopted (1881) as the provisional boundary. At the point where Sělângor,
Sungei Ujong, and Jélébu meet is the hill *Perhentian Rimpûn* (Berhim-
pûn) said to be so named from the assembly of the Chiefs of the old
" Four States."

It is with Sungei Ujong that communication has hitherto been best maintained. Some parts of Jĕlĕbu will probably be found most accessible from Sungei Lui in Sĕlângor; and other parts may be more easily approached from Malacca by way of the valley of the River Langkap, one of the head-waters of the Ulu Moar, which runs down the southern side of the Brimbûn towards Tĕrâchi.

The geology and physical geography of this State is alone of any present consequence. What political importance it possesses is derived from its position in the angle between the Protected States of Sĕlângor and Sungei Ujong, and from lying on the Pahang watershed.

Inhabitants, Products, &c.—The population is at present extremely scanty, probably not 700, being less than two to the square mile.

The only industry, beyond the cultivation of a little rice chiefly in the Klawang valley, is some tin-mining carried on by 70 Chinese at Jĕlondong near the Triang and close to the Pĕnghûlu's place, Kwâla Glâmi. The tin-deposits lie on the Pahang side of the country, and are reported to be rich and easily worked, enabling the miners to make an average output of two *bharas* a year each.

The River Triang, of which the head-waters may almost be said to form the State of Jĕlĕbu, is an important feeder of the River Pahang, and both the main stream and its largest tributary (the Kĕnâboi) are found to be deep and navigable for most of the year. Paddy is thus imported easily and cheaply from Pahang. The tin-deposits in the Kĕnâboi, Jĕlondong, Kwâla Glâmi. &c. are said to be unusually rich. Once there is better communication for its mineral exports through Sungei Ujong, there seems good prospect of this small State not only being developed itself, but playing an important part in opening up Pahang:

The State has always been one of the Nĕgri Sĕmbîlan, ruled like the rest by an elective Dato' Pĕnghûlu, with a Yam Tûan whose only function seems to be to represent the hereditary and monarchical principle.

Johol.

The old State of Johol included the whole of the country to the interior of Rĕmbau, Malacca and Sĕgâmat, containing the now separate States of Jĕlei or Inas, Sri Mĕnanti or Ulu Moar, and Jĕmpol.

The four Bâtins, or aboriginal chiefs, were he of Klang, of Jĕlĕbu, of Sungei Ujong, and of Johol (now of Moar) under whom is the Bâtin of Jĕlei.

It is stated by the natives, and it seems probable, that the former boundaries of Johol were Mount Ophir (*Gûnong Lĕdang*), and from there Rantau Pait * on the Moar a little above Kwâla Pâlong (towards Johor), thence to Lûbok Sĕrampang on the Sĕrting (towards Pahang), thence to the Jĕlĕbu boundary at Jâwi-Jâwi Bĕtâub on the river Triang,

---

* The course of the River Gĕmas, in much the same line, has, for many years, been adopted.

and from there to Sungei Langkap in Ulu Moar, and along Gûnong
Brimbûn (towards Sungei Ujong) to Bâtu Gâjah in the Pâbei pass
(towards Rêmbau).

The present State of Johol is of little consequence, the population
being extremely scanty—not more than 5,000. It is an undulating country without either large streams or high hills, and though known to contain much gold, especially on the Gêmas (*Sungei Mas* or gold river?) near
which are Chêndras and Tâon, there are no workings at present.

One of the principal districts is Inas or Jêlei, at one time perhaps
a separate State of the Nêgri Sêmbîlan, which bears the name of a river
in Johol, with which it may now be considered to be incorporated.

The Johol and the Inas both flow into the Jêlei, which falls into the
Moar. The lower part of the Jêlei stream is claimed by Johol, so that
it is a sort of little Switzerland, enclosed by Rêmbau, Sri Mênanti, Johol,
and Tampin. The direction is South-East of Sri Mênanti.

Sri Mênanti.

Sri Mênanti, as recognised in the Agreement with Government of
1876, contains about 300 square miles, and a population of about 3,000.
It is the old State of Ulu Moar with the addition of Jêmpol to the East.
The open valleys of Bandul and Têrâchi, watered by the upper stream of
the Moar, lead from Bukit Pûtus, the frontier of Sungei Ujong, to Sri
Mênanti. This was formerly, as its name implies, the seat of the Yam
Tûan or Mênangkâbau Prince, whose titular pretensions made a kind of
bond between the various free States of the Nêgri Sêmbîlan confederacy.

The country is chiefly flat, and comprises the valleys mentioned above,
in which rice is grown ; and some hill country about the sides of Gûnong
Pasir and *Perhentian Tinggi*, which is the natural boundary towards
Rêmbau. The pass across it, connecting the two States, is about 1,150
feet high. There is frequent communication between these two States.

Sri Mênanti is tolerably prosperous, though, as in all the Nêgri Sêmbîlan, its rice-crops have, for many years, been faring badly. About 500
Chinese carry on tin-mining at Bêting and Kwâla Pilah, the deposits
being found in a more open and less hilly situation than usual, carried
down, probably, from the Jêlêbu mountains.

If Jêlêbu is of more consequence in regard to its physical than its
political relations, it is just the opposite with Sri Mênanti, the position
of which is nothing if not political. It was without a Chief for some
years before the treaty of 1876. Those whose privilege it was to make a
selection could not, among the numerous claimants, make up their
minds who had the best title.

After our military occupation of this State in 1876, and upon the
withdrawal of our troops, the office of Yam Tûan. which seems to have
been in abeyance, was re-established ; and, by the treaty of that year,
Tunku Antah was given the administration of Sri Mênanti, and a general
authority over the other small States, which have not been separately
described.

Rěmbau, originally an offshoot of Sungei Ùjong, has long been one of the most populous and important of these small interior States, especially in so far as Malays are concerned. It is known, by enumeration of houses in 1884, to contain 12,000 inhabitants, almost all Malayan. Area about 400 square miles.

It is not only the best known, but is, in every respect, at present the most important of all these small States, especially in its population and in its independence of spirit. Physically speaking, Rěmbau is but an extension of the plain of Malacca, with no natural boundaries, except at one or two points, to separate the two countries. In fact, until fifty years ago, the portion of Malacca nearest to Rěmbau, called *Náning*, was itself an independent State. It has never shown the least desire to revert to its former condition. Except perhaps to the tribal heads, or *Lěmbága*, the transfer can have mattered little.

Products, Inhabitants, &c.—The inhabitants are now mainly of Sumatran race, and immigrated principally in the seventeenth century, for reasons unknown. They probably reached Rěmbau by the Linggi river, although their tradition says by the Malacca river and Náning. The principal and almost exclusive industry of the country is and has always been padi-planting, for which its heavy rainfall is an advantage. In recent years, tapioca has been cultivated by the Chinese, which has materially increased the prosperity of its people. Tin is known to exist in some quantity, especially in the river Pědas, but the prejudices of the people have hitherto prevented mining.

The soil and physical configuration of Rěmbau generally resemble those of Náning. The country is of an undulating character, the depressions being mostly planted with "sáwah," or wet padi-fields. Bukit Běsar is the only mountain in the country, exclusive of the ranges which divide it from Sungei Ujong, Sri Měnanti and Johol.

The padi-fields are extensive, but are now a good deal out of cultivation, owing to the fatal cattle disease which has raged during the last three years, and has carried off almost all the buffaloes.

Boundaries.—The boundaries of Rěmbau are not very well defined. Those with Malacca territory are the places named in the Treaty of the 9th January, 1883, and the Rěmbau branch of the Linggi, above Sempang.

The boundary with Sungei Ujong was fixed in 1881 as follows :— from Sempang to Bukit Mandi Angin, Pěrhentian Tinggi, and Gûnong Angsi.

The boundary on the inland side towards Sri Měnanti and Johol has shifted from time to time ; Gûnong Pásir, which is now under Sri Měnanti, is claimed as properly belonging to Rěmbau, though in NEWBOLD's time (1833) it was said to have originally belonged to Johol ; this is confirmed by the aborigines, who are perhaps the best authorities on such a point. The boundaries with Sri Měnanti are said to be Gûnong Tûjoh, and Gûnong Lîpat Kâjang, and those with Johol, Bâtu Gâjah and Gûnong Dato'.

Places.—Sempang deserves first mention. Here the Rĕmbau and Pĕnar join and form the Linggi, and a Police Station stands in the angle thus formed, on some land ceded to Government in 1874. It was formerly one of the chief places in Rĕmbau. Kwâla Pĕdas, a few miles up the Rĕmbau on the right bank, was another; but both these districts have been deserted. In the same way, the capital is not easy to define, for each successive Pĕnghûln seems to have his own. Bandar Râ-au was the residence of the Yam Tûan Mûda, and latterly of the ex-Pĕnghûlu, Haji Saîl. In 1837, Newbold said the Pĕnghulu resided at Chĕmbong : the present Pĕnghûlu resides at Gemayun near Chĕngkau.

Government, &c.—The Government of Rĕmbau is the best type of the tribal system to be found in the Peninsula. In something like its present form, it probably came over with the earliest immigrants from Sumatra, and has since been maintained with great conservatism among the twelve Sukus or tribes. It is by and among the *Lĕmbâga*, or hereditary chiefs of these tribes, that the Pĕnghûlu must be elected. This election follows very minute and elaborate rules, grafted by the Sumatran immigrants upon the aboriginal system, of one feature of which the following is a summary :—

" Bĕduanda is the name of one of the chief aboriginal tribes in the South of the Peninsula, and two of the chief Rĕmbau clans bear the same name—the Bĕduanda Jâwa, and the Bĕduanda Jakun—from which the Pĕnghûlu is alternately elected.

" This alternate election is said to be due to a dispute between the two branches of the Bĕduanda, over the right to elect the Pĕnghûlu, which was settled by the sovereign of Johor giving each the right alternately.

" At the same time, he gave distinctive titles to the Pĕnghûlus—to the one elected from the ' Bĕduanda Jawa ' that of ' Sădia Raja,' to him of the ' Bĕduanda Jakun ' that of ' Lêla Maharaja.' "

The office of Lĕmbâga, or electoral chief, is hereditary, descending on the side of the sister, as in Nâning and all the Mĕuangkâbau States.

PAHANG.

Pahang, between Tringgânu and Johor. extends along the eastern side of the Peninsula from 2° 40' to 4° 35' North, and has about 130 miles of sea-coast on the Gulf of Siam. Its boundaries are the River Chĕrâting. with Tringgânu : the River Ĕndau, with Johor ; and a line* along the eastern frontier of the States Jĕlĕbu, Sĕlângor and Pĕrak to the West. To the North-West the boundary is not defined. but may be taken as following the watershed of the Ulu Pahang.

Extent, &c.—Its area probably exceeds 10,000 square miles, and its line of greatest length, from Ulu Ĕndau to Ulu Pĕrak, approaches 200 miles. far exceeding the length of any such line which can possibly be drawn in any other State of the Peninsula. Besides the territory on the mainland, Pahang includes two chains of islets running parallel to its

---

* The mountain range divides Pahang and Sĕlângor : and a supposed line across the River Triang at Sungei Dûa, below Kwala Glâmi, forms the provisional boundary (1884) with Jĕlĕbu.

coast, generally at about 25 miles distance. The State of Pahang, apart from these islands, is almost identical with the basin of the river of the same name, in an even greater degree than is the case with Pêrak. This river is shallow and, therefore, not the largest in volume; yet, as regards its position in the very centre of the Malay Peninsula, and the extent of country it drains—from 3° to 5° North—the River Pahang may fairly be considered the principal stream in the whole Peninsula.

Pahang is, in many respects, the least known, geographically and otherwise, of all the Malay States, and it offers a most interesting field for exploration. The country is at once that which has the highest mountains, and the widest extent of lakes and marshes.

Mountains, &c.—The highest summit in the Peninsula is believed to be Gûnong Tahan,* which has not been ascended, or even seen by Europeans except at a great distance, but which, it is almost certain, reaches a height of between 10,000 and 12,000 feet. This is the highest point of a range which is the real back-bone or central chain of the Peninsula at its widest point. It is situated to the East of the upper waters of the River Pahang, and can probably be best reached from the Ulu Têmling (or *Têmbêliang*), a feeder of the Pahang, near Jêlei. The geological formation of the hills consists, so far as is known, of granite, sandstone, shale, and clay. Some of the islands, as Tioman and Tinggi, consist partly or entirely of trap rock.

The next highest summit is to be found on the opposite side of the Pahang valley, in the neighbourhood of Gûnong Rája, near the Sêlângor boundary. Other high hills are found in the eastern chain, from which flows the River Chêrâting (called the Sêrting near its source), the Tringgânu river *Dûngûn*, and the Kêlantan river *Lêbih*: and in the Bertangga hills, further South, on the right bank of the river Pahang, which is believed to supply the Chêno Lakes. There is, still further South, another high hill from which the Rumpen flows—Gûnong Gayong.

The Chêno lakes, and the others in the neighbourhood, as, in fact, the water system of the country generally, are peculiar to Pahang. The Pahang River drains a great length of country, as explained above, and, in its course, receives important feeders from the most opposite directions—from the mountains to the North, the South, and the West. The lower part of the stream, below Kwâla Bêrâ, flows for nearly 100 miles due East, through a very flat and marshy country. The river and its feeders here become wide and shallow, opening out into spaces like small lakes. The country between Pahang and Rumpen is particularly level, and the three main tributaries from that region—the Bêrâ, the Chêno, and the Chêni—are all noted for such lakes. That of the Bêrâ is the largest sheet of inland water in the Peninsula, but its shores, like the Chêni, are only inhabited by *Sakei*. The Chêno lakes, on the contrary, are inhabited by Malays.

The shallowness of the Pahang makes it navigable for small craft only, except in the wet season; and this feature is reproduced in the other

---

* It is said to be 50 miles from Jêlei, and is probably somewhat further North than it appears in the Straits Asiatic Society's map.

rivers of the State—the Rumpen and the Kwantan: and in the large tributaries of the Pahang—the Triang, the Sěmantan and the Lipis.

The whole coast of Pahang is, like most of the East coast of the Peninsula, an almost uninhabited forest: but it has the advantage of a fine sandy shore, with numerous *Rú* trees (*Casuarina littorea*), so that it is possible, and in the North-East monsoon not uncommon, for long journies to be undertaken along this natural road. Such a thing is nowhere possible on the West coast, with its matted jungle of mangroves and its muddy foreshore.

Inhabitants, Products, &c.—Pahang is far from being a populous country, even according to the low standard of the Peninsula, but there are a good many prosperous Malay settlements, and not least in the extreme interior. In fact, the River Lipis, an upper feeder of the Pahang, which flows down from the mountains of Ulu Sělāngor, as also the districts of Jělei and Těmling, a little further down the main stream, are said to be more thickly inhabited than any other part of the country. The Malays may be put at 50,000 for the whole of Pahang: the Chinese miners and shop-keepers at 10,000: and the Sakei, who are believed to be numerous in the unexplored southern region, at 3,000. The total is thus some 63,000 in all, or a population of about 7 to the square mile.

The chief importance of Pahang lies in its mineral wealth; its reputation for *gold* and *tin* combined being unrivalled, both for the metals' wide-spread yield, their quantity, and their fineness. .

The principal gold mines are in the valley of the Pahang at Lipis, Jělei, Sěmantan, and Lûet: gold is also found as far South as tho Běrâ. There is also a mine of *galena* on the Kwantan at Sungei Lěmbing; and tin is found throughout the country, both in the neighbourhood of the gold mines above mentioned, and in places like the River Triang and the River Běntong, where gold is not worked.

Of the "mineral" States, Pahang is, by the Malays, placed first, and Kělântan next to Pahang, and then Patâni; all these, and these alone, have galena as well as gold and tin. Gold is found in Pahang almost exclusively in the central line of the State—at Paso on the Běrâ, at Lûet, the Jělei, the Kělau, the Lipis and its feeder the Raub, &c. Whatever the explanation may be, it is worth noticing here, as it has been noticed before, that the principal gold-workings of the Peninsula lie almost entirely along a not very wide line drawn from Mounts Ophir and Sěgâmat (the southern limit of the auriferous chain) through the very heart of the Peninsula, to the Kalian Mas, or gold diggings, of Patâni and Tělěpin in the North. The best tin-workings of Pahang lie near the Sělângor hills on the River Běntong, and near the famous gold-workings at Jělei and Talom. Pahang tin is said to be the only tin on the East coast which can rival that of Pěrak and Sělângor in whiteness and pliancy.

The vegetable products are almost confined to rice and jungle produce. Pahang is said to grow sufficient rice for its own consumption, but, except the little required for Jělěbu, it cannot, like Kělantan, export any. The rice which is grown is mostly wet rice, and the buffalo is used here—

not the bullock as in the Northern States. Pahang belongs, in these respects, as in the non-domestication of the elephant, to the South rather than the North of the Peninsula.

Principal Places. —The capital of the State is Pěkan, a few miles from the mouth of the River Pahang. The other chief places in the country are Chěno, some way up the main River, Těměrělo near the River Sěmantan; Tanjong Běsar on the River Lipis; and Jelei, the gold-mining centre.

The inland communications of the country are chiefly by means of the wide-spreading river system. There are no roads, and the jungle tracks of any importance are confined to the inland connections with Kělantan and Tringgánu, &c., a way that crosses from Ulu Kwantan (by Přim, a "tin" place) to Ulu Lûet (by Sungei Gárum, a "gold" place), and another from Ulu Běrá (by Paso, a "gold" place) to Ulu Kératong, a feeder of the River Rumpen.

Government. —The government of Pahang is, practically speaking, independent and arbitrary. The State has always looked to the South—formerly to Johor, and of late years to Singapore—for support and protection, especially against Siam. But the Běndahára, who has recently assumed the title of Sultan, always exercised despotic power in his own country. About the revenue of Pahang nothing is known, but it is probably small; the country, for all its natural wealth, being entirely undeveloped. The Běndahára is the chief trader, and the Chinese settlers are but few in number compared with those of Kělantan or Johor.

The history of Pahang is obscure, and was chiefly concerned in old days with invasions and threats from Siam and, it is said, Malacca. To a great extent, Pahang escaped the troubles which Johor suffered, directly and indirectly, through its European neighbours—the Portuguese and the Dutch. Of late years, there is little to notice beyond the fact that, unlike the other States, it has been growing more instead of less independent. The present ruler, then styled Wan Ahmed, attained his position, after being opposed by force for some years, in 1862; when a Treaty with Johor was made under the sanction of the Straits Government. By virtue of this, in 1868 the long-disputed boundary with Johor—at the River Endau—was settled by the arbitration of the Governor. There has thus been created some dependence on the part of Pahang, and on the part of the Colony some obligation of protection and recognition.

JOHOR.

Johor (*Jehór*), which comprises Muar since 1877, includes the whole of the southern end of the Malay Peninsula, stretching from latitude 2° 40′ South to Cape Romania (*Rom 'nia*), and including the small islands that lie along the coast to the South of 2° 40′. It is surrounded on three sides by the sea; on the fourth side its boundaries are :— Malacca, Jèbol and the River Endau.

Extent, &c. —The area of Johor must be nearly 9,000 square miles, and its population is about 100,000, thus giving about 11 to the square mile. The population is almost confined to the districts lying near

Singapore on the one side, and Malacca on the other; the interior of the country being covered for the most part by virgin forest, only partially explored. During the last twenty-five years it has been, to some extent, opened up under its present ruler, Maharaja ABUBAKER, K.C.S.I., G.C.M.G., the descendant of the former hereditary Temenggongs. Though Johor is not possessed of the rich mineral resources of most of the other States, yet by the security of its position in the close neighbourhood of Singapore, and through its present Chief's just rule, and his care for life and property, Johor has attained some prominence, and exceptional prosperity amongst the Native States of the Peninsula.

Towns.—The capital is the town of *Johor Bháru* or *New Johor*, as distinguished from *Johor Láma* or *Old Johor*, the former seat of the Sultans of Johor, which was situated a few miles up the wide estuary of the Johor River. The new town is a flourishing little place on the nearest point of the mainland to Singapore, separated from the island by the old Straits, and lying about 14 miles to the North-East of Singapore city, in 1° 29' North. It contains some 15,000 inhabitants, mostly Chinese, who are within immediate reach of Singapore by a frequent service of conches. There is no other settlement in Johor which can be spoken of as a town; but one or two populous and flourishing villages are found on the south bank of the large River Moar, at Lénga and Bukit Kěpong. Padang, a little to the South of the River Moar, is another important and very populous place. Like Johor Bháru, it is not situated up any river, as almost every other important Malay settlement is throughout the Peninsula, but on the sea-shore, which is here exceptionally sandy and open. Padang has a population of nearly 2,000, mostly Javanese, scattered along the coast, engaged in planting and fishing.

Lénga lies about 10 miles, and Bukit Kěpong still further, up the River Moar. There are in these, as in most places in this district, many Javanese and others engaged in planting pepper, with some Chinese gambier-planters. In the North of Johor, the population is, however, chiefly Malayan, and looks to Malacca as its capital. The settlement at Kwála Sěgámat is an open and well-populated district in the interior.

Rivers.—There are three tolerably large rivers—the Moar, the Endau and the Johor—and several smaller ones, of which the Bátu Pahat and the Sědili alone need be named. The largest of all the Johor rivers is the Moar on the West coast, which is, in fact, the most important stream in the South of the Peninsula. Its upper waters have already been referred to in treating of the States known as the Něgri Sěmbilan, among which it takes its rise, flowing South-West from Brimbún (*Běrěmbün*). The population is chiefly found on the southern side of the stream, in Johor proper, of which it was formerly the natural boundary.

The other large rivers are the River Endau on the East coast, which forms the boundary with Pahang and flows down from the Sěgámat Hills; and the River Johor on the South, which flows from Mount Blúmut, and opens out into a wide estuary opposite the eastern side of the island of Singapore.

Mountains.—The country is, as a whole, less mountainous than any other part of the Peninsula. Its hills are all detached groups, or portions of two interrupted chains, running along the West and East sides respectively: the one from Mount Ophir by Pänggälam and Mount Formosa to Pûlei and the Carimons group (a geological extension of Johor); and the other from the Sëgámat Hills and Mount Janing to the Blâmut and the neighbouring hills beyond (Mëntähak and Pantî).

The Blâmut hills (3,390 feet) are the principal mountain group in Johor; giving rise to the River Johor flowing South, the River Sëdili flowing East, and the River Kahaug flowing North—to join the Sëmbrong, an affluent of the River Ëndau.

Mount Ophir, in Moar, 4.050 feet, is, probably, the highest peak in the State. It was a few years ago reckoned the highest in the Peninsula, but this is now, of course, known to be entirely erroneous. Its shape, and its situation near the sea, are remarkable. No rivers of any size take their rise in it; but two of its streams, though small, are of some consequence as marking Johor's northern boundary—the River Chohong, which, with Kësang, divides it from Malacca; and the River Gëmas, which forms its Johol boundary.

Inhabitants and Products.—The whole population of the State, including Moar, is probably over 100,000, and is remarkable for containing a larger number of Chinese than of Malays. The exact numbers have not been ascertained. It is probable that more than half the population is, to be found within 15 miles of the Singapore Straits. The Chinese are chiefly found as cultivators of gambier and pepper, spread over about this range of country in the extreme southern end of the Peninsula, nearest to Singapore, of which Johor has been described as the "back country." These cultivators go from Singapore, the capitalists for whom they cultivate are Singapore traders, and all their produce and most of their earnings find their way back to Singapore again. European pioneers have, in the last few years, made some experiments in planting, on a large scale, sago, tobacco, coffee, tea, and cocoa. These have been grown in six different districts—Bâtu Pahat, Pulau Kokob, Pûlei, Pantî, Johor Bhâru and Panggërang; but none of them have yet been planted long enough to be considered established industries. The busy collection of gutta which went on in Johor for the Singapore market, from Dr. Montgomerie's discovery of its useful properties in 1842 until the supply was exhausted, deserves special mention; as also the successful working of some large saw-mills for utilising the great resources of the country in serviceable timber, which are now, however, appreciably diminished. At the present time, the principal exports of Johor are the carefully-cultivated gambier, pepper and tapioca; and the natural products of timber, rattans and damar. For almost all such produce, Singapore is . . . . . t of shipment.

Minerals.—The only mineral in which the country is really rich is iron. It is nowhere worked, but is found almost everywhere. Some deposits of tin are known in several places, and gold in one or two spots. It is said that tin-mining is discouraged. A little is worked at Sëlûang, but no considerable mining is actually carried on, unless the islands of the Carimons be included. Though now politically separated from Johor, they are geologically part of it, and were formerly a dependency of the kingdom.

Government, &c.—The form of government is that of the usual Malay autocracy; but the freedom and the *laisser-faire* of its administration are in marked contrast with the usual administrative system of Malay States: rather resembling that of the neighbouring Colony, with which it is so closely connected both in the present and the past.

The Maharâja's Chinese subjects are by nature indifferent to their ruler, provided their personal independence is secure. Hitherto they have usually proved contented and obedient subjects to the Malay Râjas, even where their race is in a very large majority. This is true of other States as well as Johor—the miners' settlements alone excepted, such as Lûkut (1834) and Lârut (1872).

Johor has a history which extends back to the Portuguese days. It took an important part, only second to that of Achin, in the 140 years' struggle over Malacca, between the Portuguese and the Dutch. At the beginning of this century, the central authority of the Johor Sultanate having been removed from the mainland to the Lingga *(Linyin)* and Rio *(Riau)* Archipelagoes, little cohesion remained among the different feudatories. Thus, the hereditary Bendahâra (in Pahang), and the hereditary Temënggong of Johor (in Bûlaug) had virtually become independent chiefs. The titular authority of the Sultan over them was little more than a survival of the past, though at times it might suit a superior foreign power to magnify it. The Dutch, for example, when onsted from Malacca in 1795, and debarred, by the issue of the Great War, from all hopes of returning there, sought to make some settlement in the Straits. They had already taken Rio under their protection, and they now took possession of the Carimons and other islands as subject territory. Consequently, the Temënggong removed from Bûlaug to the Singapore River, where he established himself a few months before the expedition to Java (July, 1811). After the restoration of the Dutch possessions at the Peace, all the former dependencies of Johor, including Bûlaug and the Carimons, were comprised, somewhat questionably, in the Netherlands-India dominions; the Johor rule being thereafter confined to the mainland and closely adjacent islets.

The principal changes since then have been those resulting from the establishment of Singapore: from the Treaty of 1855 by which the *de facto* administrative rights of the Temënggong were acknowledged and Johor Bhâru became the capital: and from the re-union, as in former times, of the northern district of Moar to Johor in 1877. The ruler has enjoyed the new title of Maharâja, not previously known in Malaya, since 1868.

THE STRAITS SETTLEMENTS. *

The Colony of the Straits Settlements, which comprises Singapore, Penang (with Province Wellesley and the Dindings), and Malacca, now contains about 1,500 square miles, and nearly 500,000 inhabitants. The Settlements were transferred from the control of the Indian Government to that of the Secretary of State for the Colonies on the 1st April, 1867, by an Order in Council issued under 29 & 30 Vict., c. 115.

The earliest Settlement was Penang, which was founded in 1786. Its foundation is something more than the commencement of the Colony, for it marks the beginning of the enormous trade, and was in some sense the forerunner of all the colonising enterprise, in the parts beyond India—Malaya, China and Australia. It may be noticed that, within a few months of the time Captain Light first anchored in Penang harbour, the earliest expedition to Botany Bay arrived at Port Jackson. When in 1796 Penang became the Penal Station for India, there was some superficial resemblance between the two infant Settlements, and the enterprises which have both developed so enormously during the present century. The immediate prosperity of Penang, and its superiority to the Company's trading Station at Bencoolen, attracted Chinese traders, and still more Chinese settlers, and gave an early impulse to the expansion of its commerce. The troubled times of the great European War, which commenced seven years after the foundation of Penang, brought special opportunities; and at the close of a single generation the little Settlement had become a power in Malaya, under the direct and indirect influence of which the Dutch "monopoly system" had been overthrown. The British possession of the Straits after 1795, became quite secure; first through our holding Malacca, and when that was given back by the establishment of Singapore.

The Settlements were not formed into one Government till 1826. But the Straits have, since 1795, been, in every sense, a British possession, our power being paramount on the western or navigable shore.

Industries, &c.—The Colony has hitherto been little more than a place of trade; and though it is now beginning to show some development in other directions, yet, from its circumstances, trade must always be its principal feature. As a market alone, it ranks, next to Hongkong and Malta, not only above all other Crown Colonies, but with a gross total of Imports and Exports which, excluding those two Trade centres only, exceeds that of all other such colonies put together. For 1885 its total trade was $221,801,000, or over £45,000,000, giving the extraordinary rate of about £85 a head of the population. This rate exceeds that of either the United Kingdom or its most prosperous Colonies in Australia, and probably of any other Country in the world.

The early prosperity of the Colony's trade resulted from its central position as a port of call for European, Indian and Chinese trade. The local trade, for which both Singapore and Penang are so well placed, and

* Fuller particulars, especially of the Colony's history, will be found in Chapter VIII.

which now forms so much more secure a basis of future prosperity, has taken time to develope. But within the last few years, it has rapidly assumed increased proportions, and already far exceeds the ocean-going trade. At the Transfer, the United Kingdom trade with the Colony (for 1868) was £3,476,000, and the local trade (including Netherlands India and the Malay Peninsula) £2,669,000 : but now the position is reversed : the United Kingdom trade (for 1882) amounts to only £6,926,000, while there is a local trade of £10,109,000.

A similar change is seen to be in progress, on a smaller scale, in the trade with India, as compared with the essentially local trade with the Malay Peninsula. This is seen by comparing again the totals for the years 1868 and 1882 :—

	1868.	1882.
Indian trade,	...£1,968,000	£3,803,000
Malay Peninsula trade,	...£ 839,000	£3,799,000

With these facts established, there can be little to fear from any change in ocean routes. The Colony will find its surest guarantee of continuing prosperity in the growing proportions of the trade done with its immediate neighbours—those numerous and rising countries briefly referred to in Chapter VII—for which its situation makes it the natural metropolis.

Population.—The population of the Colony was, according to the Census of 1881, 423,381; and if the rate of increase during the last decennial period is maintained, it should, before the close of 1885, reach 500,000. There is good reason to believe that it is, in fact, increasing at a still more rapid rate. The population in 1856 was 248,000, and will thus have doubled itself in a generation. The Chinese and the Malays numbered alike at the last Census—the Chinese 174,327, and the Malays 174,326. It is probable that the Chinese will be in a large majority at the next enumeration.

The Chinese and Indian population have been increased, and in fact can only be maintained at their present figures, by immigration, for the women number but a fourth of the men. Among the Malays, the sexes are almost equal in number; and the increment, which in their case amounts to 2 per cent. per annum, is a natural increase, due to a high birth rate and not dependent on immigration.

Vegetable and Mineral Products.—The *flora* of the Colony is very rich in variety of forms. The number of flowering plants has been estimated at about 5,000, and the flowerless kinds at about 300; but a great number of the flowering kinds produce inconspicuous blossoms, and so are commonly supposed to be without flowers.

The kinds of trees number about 1,000: which is 1,000 *less* than are found in India, and 960 *more* than are found in Europe. The number of trees producing valuable timber may be put at 100 kinds, of which the following are considered among the best and are therefore the most commonly in use, viz. :—Balau, tampinis, seraya, meranti, daru, kladang, kûlim, petaling, rengas, merbau, &c.

As to fruit trees, native fruits of about nine varieties are in daily use, supplemented by about six introduced kinds : the latter including the pineapple, orange, &c.

The culinary vegetables are chiefly acclimatised Chinese kinds, comprising lettuces, beans, radishes, &c. of a much inferior sort to the similar European vegetables.

The vegetable products which form part of the exports of the Colony are about 40 in number, of which pepper, sugar, tapioca, indigo, coffee, cocoa-nuts, sago, gutta-percha, caoutchouc and canes are the principal.

The well-known Malacca cane is not, however, found in Malacca (as the " Penang Lawyer " is, or was, in Penang), but only in Sumatra and Borneo.

Gutta Percha (Gñtah) deserves special mention. The plants that produce it, of a commercial standing, are about 20 in number ; about 10 of which are trees, and 10 creepers ; Gñtah Tuban, the produce of a tree, being the best known.

The Straits sago is chiefly produced by a large palm which grows in swampy places, from the pith of which sago is made. The kinds of oil exported are five in number, among which an essential oil, extracted from the lemon-grass, is the most important. Tea, coffee and chocolate are not yet produced in large quantities. Among spices, nutmegs, cloves, pepper and cinnamon are exported : the pepper in large quantities, though most of it is not grown in the Colony.

The grape-vine is not found native in the Colony, and only succeeds with great difficulty under cultivation. Native vines with clusters which rival those of the grape-vine in beauty, but are uneatable, are however found in great plenty.

Of late years, both public and private enterprise have been active in introducing various foreign plants which yield valuable products : among more recent ones may be enumerated the teak tree of India, the Brazil-nut tree, and American and African Indian-rubber producing trees. The Queensland-nut bush and numerous other useful and European plants are being tried on the hills, with more or less success.

A curious feature of the vegetation of the Colony is the appearance of many Australian plants on the higher hill tops. The beautiful Victoria regia lily of the Amazon grows well, and many other introduced plants have become acclimatised in gardens and by the way-side ; but owing to the stimulating nature of the climate, few of them produce flowers or fruit as freely as in their native habitat, while leaves and branches flourish much more freely.

Many products, once abundant in the Colony, have become comparatively rare, through wasteful habits and the want of any systematic conservation ; in fact many have retired considerably beyond the limits of the Settlements, and the Government of the Colony has taken steps to re-establish some of these by growing young plants on waste-lands and in forest reserves.

Minerals.—No minerals are found in any workable quantities, except a little tin in the South of Malacca. This is natural from the situation of the Settlements, lying as they do upon the coast of the Straits. Almost immediately beyond the frontier, it happens that both in Province Wellesley and Malacca valuable tin deposits have been worked, and in the latter Settlement some gold-diggings also, near Mount Ophir.

Government.—The Government is of the usual type in British Crown Colonies. It is ranked as a "First Class" Colony, *i.e.*, the Governor's salary comes within the category " £5,000 and upwards." The Governor has also general control over the Protected Native States, above described (page 35).

The Colony's Revenue is now about $3,600,000 a year, and a Municipal Revenue of about $530,000 more is collected separately. The rate contributed is thus nearly £2 a head of the population, which, though lower than the rate in the Australian Colonies, stands highest among the Crown Colonies.

The Protected States have a joint Revenue of $2,355,191, which, added to that of the Colony, gives a total Revenue of over $6,000,000— an amount equal to that collected in the much larger and more populous Colony of Ceylon, which has hitherto headed the list of Crown Colonies. .

The progress which the Crown has made since the transfer, can be fairly gauged by comparing the following figures :—

	1868.	Estimated for 1885.
Singapore,	...$ 864,918	$ 2,075,383
Penang,	.. „ 824,196	„ 1,264,470
Malacca,	... „ 112,725	„ 308,215
	$ 1,301,843	$ 3,648,068

It will be seen that in revenue—and it is also the case in trade—the progress during this period has been greatest in Penang and Malacca, though Singapore easily maintains its position as the Capital.

SINGAPORE.

SINGAPORE is an island about 27 miles long by 14 wide, containing an area of 206, or, with the adjacent islets, 223 square miles, situated at the southern extremity of the Malay Peninsula, in lat. 1° 17′ North, long. 103° 50′ East. It is separated from the Continent by a narrow strait. (*Sĕlat Tĕbrqu*) about three-quarters of a mile in width. All the small islands within ten miles of its shores form part of the Settlement.

The seat of Government, for the whole Colony, as well as the Settlement, is the town of Singapore, at the south of the island, in lat. 1° 17′ North, and long. 103° 50′ East.

Singapore was taken possession of by Sir STAMFORD RAFFLES, with the consent of the Governor-General, in February, 1819, under an agreement with the Princes of Johor. It was at first left in his charge, he being then Lieutenant-Governor of Bencoolen in Sumatra; but in 1823, it was transferred to the direct Government of Bengal. It was afterwards, in 1826, incorporated with Penang and Malacca, and placed under the Governor and Council of the incorporated Settlement. It became the recognised seat of Government in 1837.

The surface of the island is undulating, nowhere over 500 feet high, and consisting of laterite resting on sandstone. Granite is found in a few places, principally to the North and East. Gambier, indigo, pepper and many local fruits and vegetables grow well; but the Settlement depends for rice on the neighbouring countries of Java, Saigon, Burma and Bengal.

Its population, according to the Census of 3rd April, 1881, was 139,208 ; comprising 2,769 Europeans, 22,114 Malays, 86,766 Chinese, and 12,104 Natives of India.

PENANG.

Penang is the name both of an Island, and of the Settlement for which it is the seat of local administration.

The Settlement has altogether an area of about 600 square miles. The island, officially called Prince of Wales' Island, is about 15 miles long and 9 broad, containing an area of only 107 square miles, situated off the West coast of the Malay Peninsula in 5° N. latitude, and at the northern end of the Straits of Malacca.

On the opposite shore of the mainland, from which the island is separated by a sea channel a few miles broad, lies Province Wellesley, a strip of territory containing 270 square miles, and forming part of the Settlement. The Province averages 7 miles in width, and extends 45 miles along the coast ; it includes, since the Pangkor Treaty (1874), about 25 square miles of newly acquired territory to the South of the Krian. About 200 square miles of land in the Pangkor islands and opposite coast are also comprised in the territory of the Settlement.

The chief town is George Town, in 5° 24′ North latitude and 100° 21′ East longitude. The local Government of the whole Settlement is administered by a Resident Councillor.

Its population, according to the Census of 1881, was 190,597 ; comprising 674 Europeans, 84,724 Malays, 67,820 Chinese, and 27,115 Natives of India.

MALACCA.

MALACCA is situated about one-third of the way up the western coast of the Peninsula, between Singapore and Penang, about 110 miles from the former and 210 from the latter, and consists of a strip of territory about 42 miles in length, and from 8 to 25 miles in breadth, containing an area of 659 square miles.

The principal town, called Malacca, is in 2° 10′ North latitude and 102° 14′ East longitude. The local Government is administered by a Resident Councillor.

Its population, according to the Census of 1881, was 93,579, comprising 40 Europeans, 67,488 Malays, 19,741 Chinese, and 1,887 Natives of India.

SECTION II.

BORNEO.

CHAPTER V.

GENERAL DESCRIPTION.

Borneo, so called by the early Europeans, and probably by their predecessors the Mahomedan navigators, from the name of *Brûnei* its best known principality in the China Sea, occupies nearly the centre of the Eastern Archipelago, and is almost bisected by the Equator. It lies between latitude 4° S. and 7° N., and longitude 109° and 119° E., having to the North and West the China Sea; to the East the Straits of Macassar; and to the South the Java Sea. A name by which the Malays of the Archipelago sometimes call it is *Tanah Kĕlĕmantan* (Mango Land), but among the indigenous people of Borneo, it possesses no general name.

Its greatest length lies in 115° East longitude, and follows almost exactly the line of North and South, from Point Sampan-Mangis at Marûdu Bay to Tanjong Sĕlàtan (South Point) near the River Banjer in the Residency of Banjer-Massin: this distance is just under 700 miles. Its greatest breadth lies in latitude 1° North and follows precisely the line of East and West, from Point Kanyungan in Macassar Straits to the mouth of the River Sambas, between Saràwak and Pontiànak: this distance is just over 600 miles. The shape of this great island is, therefore, almost square, and entirely unlike that of the other large islands of the world, and more especially of those in its neighbourhood. This, together with the fact of its being, next to Australia and

Greenland, the largest* piece of isolated land on the globe, will account for the enormous extent of almost uninhabited and even unexplored territory in the interior, as compared with more remote islands like Celebes and Madagascar, and, in fact, every other great island, except New Guinea and Formosa.

The area of Borneo is variously computed at from 263,000 to 290,000 square miles, † or about twelve times the size of Ceylon, seven times that of Java, and nearly four times that of Great Britain. The whole of the British Isles, including Ireland and the seas surrounding them, can be placed in Borneo without occupying more than a part of the space, as can be seen by drawing a map to scale. It has a coast-line of over 2,000 miles, which is less indented than most of the large islands of the Archipelago, the few spacious bays and deep-water harbours it possesses being in the North, where the coast is higher and more abrupt. As a rule, the shores of Borneo are bordered by a broad margin of lowland and swamp, from 30 to 50 miles broad, showing recent alluvial formation. New land, as in Landak, is known to have been gained from the sea during the last four centuries, and from other signs the coast-line of Borneo is certainly extending. Its bays are neither so deep or so numerous as to interfere with the regularity of its contour. For its size, it possesses but few really navigable rivers, all that

* The area of New Guinea has been recently computed at 312,000 square miles, or some 40,000 in excess of Borneo, but its very outline is still uncertain.

† There has been some confusion as to this area, partly through the use of *mile* in different senses. In the new *Encyclopædia Brittanica* it is said that "its whole area is "estimated by MELVILLE VON COENBEE at 12,745 square miles." In KEITH JOHNSTON's *Physical Geography* (1880) it is stated—"its length is more than 800 miles "N. to S.; its breadth is more than 600 miles E. to W." In WALLACE's *Australia* (1879)—"its length is more than 850 English miles; its breadth is more than 800 "English miles." The true figures are:—greatest length N. to S. from Point Sampau-Mangi at Marudu Bay to South Point (Tanjong Selatan), 690 miles; greatest breadth E. to W. from Point Kanyungan to the mouth of the River Sambas, 605 miles. Area 263,000 square miles, as measured on BRINKMAN's large Map of 1879.

flow into the China Sea having bars at their mouths, though sometimes, like the Saráwak, deep enough for local steamers. The short river or estuary of Brûnei is an exception, for it might easily be made navigable by large ships for 15 miles, and has been called, on that account, "the most useful river of the island."

Borneo is entirely surrounded by a shallow sea of under 50 fathoms, and its coast thus enjoys tolerable calm in both monsoons. Of the interior regions of the island, a great part has been only partially explored, so that the physical features cannot be given with much precision and detail. The centre of the island seems to be occupied by a kind of table-land, with which the principal chains of mountains connect themselves. The largest of these is the Kelingkang range, parts of which are known by various local names. It traverses Borneo from Tanjong Datu in the West to Kina Balu in the North-East, in a line with the high ranges of the Philippines, further North ; while from the central region other ridges extend South (Kaminting) and South-East (Merâtu) towards the eastern angle, enclosing wide lowlands. These, if the sea were gaining on the land, instead of the reverse, would some day become gulfs like those of the adjacent island of Celebes. Mount Kina Balu (said to be 13,698 feet high) in the extreme northern corner of the island is, if it is really of that height, which has been doubted, the highest summit, not only of Borneo, but of the whole Archipelago, except perhaps the unvisited snowy peaks of New Guinea.

The island, which is abundantly supplied with rivers, may be physically divided into five principal versants. The least wide lies to the North along the China Sea, and supplies Saráwak and Brûnei. Its important rivers are the Saráwak, the

Bâtang-Lupar, the Sĕrîbas, the Rĕjang (which is navigable for
140 miles), the Bintûlu, the Baram, the Limbang or Brûnei River, the Tĕwâran, and the Tampasuk; the last two having
their sources in Mount Kina Balu itself. But by far the largest
rivers are those in the south-western versant; the largest being
the Kapûas (which, rising in 114° E. longitude, falls into the sea
between Mĕmpawa and Sukadâna) and thé Banjer-Masin or
Barîto, the master stream of this country, which rises in the
Kûtei-Lama lake, and reaches the Sea of Java at 114° East longitude, in the centre of the South coast almost opposite to Sourabaya in Java. The next largest, the Kûtei (Coti) or Mahakkan, rises in Mount Lasan-Tula, flows East with a rapid course,
and falls by numerous mouths into the Straits of Macassar.
Most of the rivers of the northern versant are necessarily short,
as the island there narrows into a kind of promontory.

Gulfs and Bays.—Datu Bight to the East of Sarâwak, Gaya
Bay, Marûdu Bay, with Kudat Harbour on the North, Paitan
Bay, Labuk Bay, Sandâkan Harbour, and Darvel Bay on the
West of British North Borneo.

Straits.—Carimata Channel between Borneo and Billiton;
Macassar Strait between Borneo and Celebes.

Capes.—Cape Samba, Flat Point, Cape Malang-Layer, and
Cape Sungei Bharu on the South; Capes Datu, Sirik, and
Baram on the East; Cape Kanyungan, Sampan-Mangio Point
on the North; Cape Unsang at the end of a promontory on
the East.

Islands.—There are very few islands of importance off the
coast of Borneo, a fact which has been explained by the
deposition of new land which is going on, many of the islands
which fringed the coast in former times having, it is supposed,

become incorporated with the mainland.) The largest is Pulau Laut at the South-East corner of the East Residency and only separated from it by a few miles. Carimata Island, on the South-West, is about 10 miles long, and lies 50 miles from the coast of Borneo: it is uninhabited, though visited by itinerant Malays who collect tortoise-shell, tripang and edible birds' nests. The Tambelan islands lie off the western extremity of Borneo, at the distance of nearly 100 miles. Off the north-western point, is the island of Great Natuna, with several smaller islets around it and nearer the coast. The inhabitants are Malays, and are under the authority of the Sultan of Lingin, and therefore under the protection of the Dutch.

The only other islands worth noting are Balambangan and Banggi (Banguey) lying 10 or 12 miles from the north-eastern extremity of Borneo. Their principal interest is historical, the East India Company having made on Balambangan its earliest Settlement in 1768, some 20 years before the settlement of Penang.

The Sooloo, or Sulu, Archipelago is a group of neighbouring islands, said to be more than 150 in number, whose inhabitants have borne an evil reputation for piracy. They are all Mahomedans of Malay race, and their Sultan has put forward claims to sovereignty over part of North Borneo and the island of Cagayan Sulu. Sulu itself is now held in dependence by the Spaniards. The pearl fisheries in its neighbourhood have long been renowned.

Mountains.—Two extensive chains may be traced, with many breaks, outlying spurs, and table-lands. The higher and more northerly runs from Cape Datu in 25° 5′ North, through the length of the island. Its different parts are

known by various names, as the Kelingkang or Bayang-Miut,
Madi, Anga-Anga Mountains; and its culminating summit
is Kina Balu. The second and more southerly chain is known
as the Kaminting Mountains. A third and fourth are known
as the Merâtu and Sakûru Mountains, respectively. These
chains all culminate towards the North-East, reaching about
6,000 feet high in that direction, and about 2,000 feet on
the western side.

Volcanoes.—Unlike most of the larger islands of the Archipelago, and in remarkable contrast with Java, Borneo possesses
no active volcano. Its southern and western shores lie over 200
miles from the nearest point of the great volcanic chain.
Many of the peaks, however, bear distinct evidence of former
activity, in what appear to have been regular craters.

The prevailing rocks are limestone, slate, sand-stone con-
glomerates, and on the mountain tops syenitic granite. It
is in the caves of the limestone hills that the edible birds'
nests are found.

Rivers.—The three largest rivers in Borneo are, as has been
stated, those which fall into the Java Sea: the Kapûas, the
river of Pontiânak, which, rising in 114° East longitude, falls
into the sea between Mĕmpawa and Sukadâna; and the Barito
or Banjer-Masin river, which rises in the Kûtei-Lama lake, and
reaches the sea at 114° East longitude, in the centre of the
South coast and almost opposite to Sourabaya in Java. Next
comes the Kûtei or Mahakkan, which rises in Mount Lasan
Tula, flows East with a rapid course, and falls by numerous
mouths into the Straits of Macassar. Among the larger
rivers on the northern side, may be named the Bâtang-Lûpar
to the East of Sarâwak; the Seríbas, the Rĕjang, a little further

East; the Baram, which enters the sea at Baram point; the Limbang or Brûnei River, on a branch of which stands the native town of that name; the Bintûlu, the Tewâran, and the Tampâsuk, the last two being in North Borneo, and having their sources in Mount Kini Balu. Besides these, there are hundreds of smaller rivers all round the coast of Bornзo, but, hardly any of them admit of the entrance of large vessels.

Lakes.—No important lakes are known in Borneo, those that exist being for the most part expansions of the rivers in the plains or flat valleys. These are generally so shallow, except in times of flood, as to be rather marshes than lakes. Among these, the much disputed Lake Balu, south-eastward of Mount Kina Balu, used to be reckoned, but its existence, as a permanent lake, has been recently disproved. Danau-Malâyu is in latitude 1° 5′ North, longitude 114° 20′ East; the length is reported to be 8 leagues, the breadth 4, and the depth 18 feet.

Climate.—The rainfall is remarkably heavy in most parts of Borneo, especially to the North-West. In Sarâwak, it averages about 180 inches. The climate, owing to this, to the influence of the sea-breezes, and to the equatorial situation of the island, is milder and more healthy than in most parts of the Archipelago. The climate of the North is similar to that of the Peninsula, not being subject to hot land-winds. The West coast has no really dry season, but is refreshed by heavy and continuous rain all the year round, especially from December to March. The mean reading of the thermometer at Pontiânak is 82°, and it never exceeds 92°. In the promontory of North Borneo, the thermometer is lower, and is found rarely to exceed 86°, although the rainfall is lower than in other part of Borneo, and seldom reaches 90 inches.

Soil.—The soil, so far as it is yet known, is not so fertile as in the volcanic islands. Much of it is still covered with a primeval forest, in which are found not only the gigantic timber trees, which the poorest soil will produce in equatorial regions, but many of the most useful tropical products, such as benzoin, camphor, gutta, the sago-palm, and the rattan. The latter grows remarkably well in the South-West, the Banjer-Masin rattan having a higher value than that of any other country in Malaya.

Dutch Settlements in Borneo.

The Dutch claim sovereignty over the greater part of Borneo, but not in any of the territory lying to the North of a line from Saráwak to the Sibuko river. They have established three Residentships—at Pontiának, Banjer-Masin and Kûtei—with the usual system of residential government, over the coast districts of the West and South. The whole southern portion, comprising more than one-fifth of the entire island, is claimed by them, and is more or less under their control, while the remaining, or northern, portion comprises the Sultanate of Borneo Proper, with Sabah (North Borneo) and Saráwak on either side.

Pontiának.

Pontiának is the name of the Western district, which comprises Pontiának, Sambas, Montrado and Sintang. It is the oldest trading settlement in Borneo and has remained under the nominal rule of a Sultan. Tin, gold and diamonds are obtained from numerous Chinese mines in this district. Sintang, on the Upper Kapúas river, is the seat of an Assistant Resident, who supervises the many tribes of Dyaks in the interior.

Banjer-Masin.

The Southern district is called Banjer-Masin; and this Residency includes Kwân and the Sub-residencies of Amuntal and Martapura, with a population of about 600,000 people, mostly Dyaks. The town of Banjer-Masin is situated about 15 miles from the mouth of the Barito. Its population is estimated at upwards of 34,000. Of the commercial community, the Chinese form the most important portion.

Kûtei.

Kûtei is the Eastern district: and at Têngárong, a Bugis settlement, 50 miles up the river Kûtei, there is an Assistant Resident. The

East coast, from Sebamban in Tanah Bambu to Kanyungan in 1° 3′ North latitude, is directly under the Dutch Government.

Places:—

Pontiának, near the mouth of Kapúas, is the town of most importance in Borneo, being the chief Dutch Settlement, with a considerable number of Chinese miners and some European residents.

Banjer-Masin, in the South-East, is a less populous town, though the capital of a larger Residency, both in extent and population.

Taborniau, the chief trading place of the South coast, is situated southward of Banjer-Masin.

Samarinda and *Téngárong*, on the Kútei river, are the most important places on the eastern side of Borneo.

English Settlements.

Saráwak.

The territory of Saráwak comprises an area of about 40,000 square miles, with a population of about 28), 1)), composed of various races, chiefly Dyaks. Saráwak now extends East and West 400 miles from Mount Mûlu (9,000) to Mount Poi (6,000). It has an average breadth inland of nearly 100 miles. It is situated on the North-West coast of the island of Borneo, and is intersected by many rivers, some of them navigable for a considerable distance inland, the largest being the Réjang, the Baram, and the Batang Lupar. The general directions of these and of the other large streams between the Saráwak and the Baram, is from East to West, or nearly parallel to the coast. The present rule has now lasted over forty years, and appears to be firmly established. The Government of the district, from Tanjong Datu to the entrance of the Samaharan river, was obtained from the Sultan of Brûnei, in September, 1841, by Mr. Brooke, who has since become better known as Rája Brooke of Saráwak. At the close of 1838, he took his yacht, the " Royalist,' to the new British Settlement of Singapore : thence he proceeded, after a short stay, to Kúching, the capital of Saráwak, to which the attention of Singapore merchants had recently been directed, owing to the discovery of antimony. He found a Brûnei Rája, Muda Hassim, installed there. Brooke was soon obliged to leave Saráwak, which was in a state of rebellion ; but in August, 1840, he returned thither, and joined Muda Hassim's party, who with Brooke's assistance overcame and dispersed the rebels. The following year he obtained his first cession of territory. In 1861, a second cession was obtained of all the rivers and land from the Samaharan river to Kadúrong point ; and in 1882 a third cession, of one hundred miles of coast-line, and all the country and rivers that lie between Kadúrong point and the Baram river, including about 3 miles of coast on the North-East side of the latter. The present Rája, H.H. Charles Johnson Brooke, is a nephew of Sir James Brooke, and succeeded in May, 1868.

The success of his experiment in administration was shown during the Chinese insurrection in 1857, when the whole indigenous population

—Malay and Dyak alike—rallied round the English Râja, drove out the rebellious miners, and triumphantly restored his power. By patience, and freedom from prejudice, the Sarâwak Government have brought peace and safety and comparative prosperity, in the place of piracy and tribal warfare and oppression. Kûching is the chief town of Sarâwak, and contains a population of about 20,000. The Râja's Palace or "Astana" is situated here, as also the Bishop's House, the ordinary residence of the Bishop of the Diocese of Singapore, Labuan and Sarâwak.

Products.—The country is rich in minerals, producing gold, silver, diamonds, antimony, quicksilver, coal, gutta-percha, india-rubber, excellent canes and rattans, camphor, bees' wax, birds' nests, sago, tapioca, pepper, and gambier. The revenue in 1882 amounted to $266,039 and the expenditure to $240,526. Value of imports and exports during 1881 was $3,666,908. The principal sources of revenue are the Opium, Gambling, Arrack and Pawn Farms, producing (1881) $91,797.

Government.—The Government of Sarâwak may be termed constitutional, its arrangements being, in their general features and effect, not unlike the constitution of a Crown Colony. The Râja is the absolute Head of the State, and retains full power of spontaneous and independent action. This power is, however, rarely exercised, and for all practical purposes of local and general government, he is guided by his Legislative Council, composed of two Europeans and five native Malay Chiefs.

A large assembly or council is periodically held, composed of the principal representatives—Native as well as European—of the several districts. It numbers between 50 and 60 members, and sits once in three years, or when specially summoned to discuss important and pressing business. Any important change in the law, or modification of native custom, would be considered by the General Council.

The Government of the various districts and outstations, forts, and rivers, is mainly entrusted to European Officers, who are termed Residents, assisted by subordinate or Assistant Residents, and by Native or Eurasian and Chinese clerks. The total number of the European staff is now about twenty.

A system of mild slavery exists in the country, but the general tendency of the Sarâwak Government has been to abolish it gradually and effectively without disturbance, and to reduce it within the narrowest limits, pending its total abolition, which is now imminent.

The capital town of Sarâwak is Kûching, situated on the Sarâwak river, about 23 miles inland, in lat. 1° 32' N. and long. 110° 28' E. This river has a bar like the others, but is navigable for small steamers. Kûching is now a place of considerable trade, conducted chiefly with Singapore. It is, as stated above, the seat of Government and the residence of some few European merchants. When Brooke became Râja, the town had only a very small population. In 1848 it was estimated at 6,000, while it has now increased to 15,000 or 20,000. It does a large trade, and is steadily growing in importance.

British North Borneo.

British North Borneo, or the territory of Sabah, obtained by a trading company from the Sultans of Brûnei and Sulu, is another singular
experiment in administration. It* extends from the Kimanis River on the
West to the Sibuco River on the East coast—an area of about 18,000
square miles, with a coast-line of about 500 miles. It is situated
nearly midway between Singapore and Hongkong, between latitude 4°
and 7° N.. and longitude 116° and 119° E., having the Sultanate of
Brûnei on the East, and Dutch Borneo on the South. Population about
200,000, composed principally of Bajaus, Ilanos, Sulus, Dusuns, &c.,
and a few Malays, and Cl inese.

The names of two enterprising gentlemen must always be mainly associated with the experiment which is being made to develope this
territory—Baron Overbeck. to whom is due the first conception of the
scheme, and Mr. Alfred Dent, who supplied the means of bringing it to
trial. The Provisional Company was established in 1877, and Her
Majesty's Charter was signed on the 1st of November, 1881. The company have formed three principal establishments, or residencies, viz.. on
the North-West coast, on the Pupar and Tampasuk rivers, and on the
East coast at Sandákan Harbour.

Towns.—Sandúkan, or Elopúra, situated in a bay of that name, the
seat of Government and the residence of the Governor ; Kudat on Marûdu, Kimánis. Papar, and Gaya on the West Coast ; and Abai on
the Tampasuk Bay.

Capes.—Cape Unsang, and Tëngku Sampan-Mangio Point in the
North.

Bays.—Marûdu, Labuk, Darvel, Ambong, Gaya, and Kimanis. This
last is one of the natural harbours of the Company's territory, said to
contain 10 square miles of good anchorage, with five to twenty fathoms of
water. It is well situated both commercially and strategically, and is
capable of being easily defended from Gaya and Sapangar Islands ; it is
not only well protected in all weather, but, lying not far from the trade
route between Hongkong and Singapore, is well suited as a place of refuge
for our merchant navy in case of warfare. There are other harbours well
suited for shelter and general shipping purposes, though strategically of less
importance than Gaya. Such are Ambong Bay on the West, Marûdu
Bay with Kûdat Harbour on the North, and Sandákan Bay on the East
coast. From the last of these, the bulk of the export trade is at present
carried on. It is the best protected harbour in Borneo, being for 20
miles almost completely land-locked ; on the other hand it is much shal-
lower than Gaya Bay. The new town Elopúra, built upon a promontory
commanding its entrance, has now become the Company's chief trading
place.

---

* Quite recently it has been extended towards Brûnei so as to include the River
Padas, and between 3,000 and 4,000 square miles of additional territory.

Rivers.—Kimanis, Papar, Tampasuk, Pandasan, Měngkábóng, Kina-batángan, and Anánam River in Gaya Bay.

Soil and Climate.—The testimony of all travellers, which is confirmed by statistics, shows that this part of Borneo is much cooler than most countries of the same latitude. The extreme summer heat is rarely over 85° in the shade; in the cool season the minimum temperature falls to 65°.

Products.—It seems probable that this territory lacks the advantage of the mines of antimony and other metals found in Saráwak, though traces of gold and of tin have been found recently; but there are known to be several extensive pearl fisheries within the Company's boundaries; and lastly, but perhaps most important of all, coal appears to exist both on the East and West coasts.

Rice, yams, sago, arrow-root, and sweet potatoes are cultivated by the natives: also the cocoa-nut, palmyra and areca palms, pepper, betel, tobacco, cocoa and coffee. The forests abound in ebony, mango, camphor-wood, and *bilían* or iron-wood; also gutta-percha, rubber, rattans, and cinnamon, are found wild.

The trade of the country at present consists mainly of the ordinary jungle produce of the eastern islands, and the only exports, as yet, are birds' nests, ebony, camphor, rattans, and sago. A powerful saw-mill is now at work at Sandákan.

Government.—The Government is administered by the Company's Governor, assisted by a Council and by Residents; and the mode of administration in a British Crown Colony is adhered to as far as practicable.

The Revenue as yet scarcely reaches $100,000; it is derived from an Opium Farm, sales of land, export and import dues, &c.

Labuan.

This English Settlement off the coast of Borneo was purchased by the British Government from the Sultan of Brûnei in 1817. The island of Labuan is situated on the North-West coast of Borneo, in 5° 16′ N. lat., and 115° 15′ E. longitude; it is 12 miles long, and at one part 5 or 6 broad, comprising an area of 30 square miles. It is distant from the coast, at the nearest point, about 6 miles, and from Brûnei, the capital of Borneo, about 30 miles.

The principal expectations of success for the new Settlement were founded upon the existence of rich coal deposits in the island, the development of which was undertaken by a Company formed in England at the time, under the name of "The Eastern Archipelago Company." Nevertheless, the coal resources of Labuan still remain comparatively undeveloped.

Labuan has a fine port, and is a market for much of the produce of the neighbouring coasts of Borneo and the Sulu Archipelago; such as bees' wax, edible birds' nests, camphor, gutta-percha, india-rubber, pearls, tortoise-shell, and trìpang, which are forwarded by the Labuan traders to Singapore.

There are three sago manufactories in the island, where the raw material received from the coast is converted into sago-flour, which is exported chiefly to the Singapore market.

The Government is administered by a Governor, under the Colonial Office, who also acts as Consul-General for Borneo under the Foreign Office. It is in every sense one of the smallest of the independent Governments under the British Crown.

The chief sources of Revenue are the farming of licenses to sell tobacco, spirits, opium in retail, and to erect fishing-stakes. The value of imports and exports in 1882 amounted to $1,251,000. The census of April, 1881, gave a population of 5,995 souls.

BRÚNEI OR BORNEO PROPER.

Brúnei is a Malay principality on the North coast, probably the most ancient of all now existing in the island, being indeed that from which it has derived its modern European name. It is situated about 14 miles from the mouth of the river Limbang, which is navigable for vessels of considerable size. This State is bounded to the East and West by its British neighbours, Sabah and Sáráwak, to the South it extends into the Dyak country from 100 to 150 miles inland, with but little authority beyond the coast. The inhabitants are mostly Mahomedans, governed by a Sultan, who is nominally absolute. The Sultan of Borneo had, until recent years, a sovereignty over the entire north-eastern coast from Saráwak to beyond Marûdu Bay. Papar, Mangedara, Paitan, and Tirun, in the North-East, are mostly Sulu settlements. The Sulus at one time held an extensive tract of country around Cape Unsang; living under the rule of the Sultan of Sulu.

The most populous and the only important town in Borneo Proper is the native city of Brúnei. Sir JAMES BROOKE called the town " a Venice of hovels." It was taken by the British in 1846, but was restored almost immediately, upon the cession of Labuan. The population of Brúnei was then stated to be 40,000, and that of the whole kingdom was put at 225,000, but both of these figures must now be considerably reduced. The population of this part of Borneo is more Malayan than of other places on this coast.

CHAPTER VI.

BORNEO.

INHABITANTS, PRODUCTS, HISTORY.

INHABITANTS.

The population of Borneo, according to the most recent statistics available, may be stated as follows :—

South-Eastern division,	... (1871)	848,166
Western division,	... (1871)	335,808
North Borneo,	... (1878)	175,000
Brunei,	(1876)	125,000
Saráwak, ...	... (1883)	250,000
Unexplored Interior,		300,000
		2,033,974

or about eight to the square mile.

The total has been estimated as high as three millions: on the other hand, some of the best of the "reference" Annuals (1881) give only 1,750,000. These compilers probably follow Mr. CRAWFURD, who, in 1856, estimated it as low as 1,800,000 and considered even that number "far above the actual population." This writer's estimates of population for Sumatra and the Peninsula have, however, on further information, proved far too low: and it may be safely assumed that the entire population of Borneo is, at this date, rather above than below 2,000,000.

Races.—The 2,000,000 inhabitants of Borneo may be divided into :—

Dyaks,	..	..	.. 1,000,000 approximately.
Malays,	..	..	.. 400,000 do.
Chinese,	..	..	.. 350,000 Dutch census 1871.
Bugis,	..	..	.. 100,000 do. do.
Javanese,	..	..	.. 100,000 do. do.
Miscellaneous (Sulus, Europeans,			
Arabs, &c.),	..	..	50,000 estimated.
			2,000,000

The aborigines of Borneo are all of Malayan race, and the most numerous are known as *Dyaks;* but they are divided into many tribes, speaking more or less distinct languages, and are distinguished by various names in different parts of the island. They differ from the Malays in being somewhat lighter, more active, and of a more trusting disposition. In the North-West the *Dusun* tribes correspond to the Land Dyaks of Saráwak, while the *Milanaus* correspond to the Sea Dyaks. The Kayans, considered to be one of the most advanced of uncivilised races, inhabit the northern interior, along the rivers Kutei, Baram and the head-waters of the Rèjang and Bintûlu. They are addicted to head-hunting, and are believed to be an intruding race, which has come from the East coast, having originally crossed from Celebes. They are heathens, and are usually tattooed.

The Malays are only found in a few centres, and those entirely confined to the vicinity of the coast, while the Dyaks occupy the greater part of the interior country. The Dyak practice of taking heads as trophies was originally common among almost all the Dyak tribes, but has now been abolished where European influence is predominant. It was observed as a custom, but it did not imply any extraordinary barbarism or moral delinquency; for it is the general opinion that the Dyaks are among the best of the class of semi-civilised tribes, being kind, truthful, and endowed with many excellent qualities. The Dyaks cultivate rice, and many kinds of vegetables, and have large plantations of fruit.

Several other races have settled in Borneo, which, from its central position, has naturally been made a resort for all the surrounding islands. The Javanese, it is said, at one time made a regular Settlement in South Borneo. This is attested by monuments still existing there, and found even as far North as the Kutei valley. The Bugis of Celebes have also considerable Settlements on the South and East of Borneo. Further North are the Settlements of the Sulus, who speak the Bisaya language of the Philippines, and who formerly held an extensive tract of country around Cape Unsang under the rule of the Sultan of Sulu. None of the indigenous people of Borneo have invented writing, while the Malays all use the Arabic character.

Among other Colonists who have settled in Borneo, must be mentioned the Chinese, who are to be found in every town on the island, either as traders, miners, mechanics, or agriculturists. They are most numerous in the western parts of the island, where gold and diamonds are found, and there are said to be nearly 350,000 Chinese in the Dutch territories alone. The trade of Saràwak, North Borneo and Labuan is, to a great extent, in their hands. But it seems probable, from old records of travel, that at one time the North-East part of Borneo was far more permanently settled by Chinese than it has been in modern times.

PRODUCTS.

The principal commerce of Borneo is carried on with Singapore and Batavia, from the northern and southern coasts, respectively. The most important part of its commerce is composed of its natural products, especially minerals. Among the mineral products are gold, which is found towards the extreme West, in Saràwak, Sambas, and Pontianak; diamonds chiefly in the same districts, and at Landak; and antimony which has been found in great abundance at Saràwak, and is perhaps the most notable of all the mineral products of Borneo. It was the discovery of this metal which indirectly led to the occupation of Saràwak (Sèráwak), for when the existence of this ore was first heard of in Singapore, it was what was then called "the Dyak Town of Serawak" that sent it. The Sambas Chiefs, who at first got the trade, in a short time despatched 1,400 tons of ore. But when it was learned that it fetched a good price in Singapore, the Brunei Chiefs, from whom Mr. BROOKE afterwards obtained Saráwak, settled there; and antimony ore has since been a regular article of export. Mercury, iron and coal are also found; the latter in several places, mines having been worked at Labuan, Sadong, &c., and at Banjer-Musin. This is the only island of the Archipelago which has yielded diamonds, the largest known being one of 307 carats. The principal diamond mines are those of Landak, about 50 miles from the Chinese territory of Pontianak. Coal is worked in several parts of the Dutch territory, and promising beds occur in Rája BROOKE's territory and in British North Borneo.

The vegetation of Borneo is exceedingly luxuriant, the whole island being, with few exceptions, one vast forest. It is especially rich in palms and forest trees, few of which have yet been botanically described. The vegetation is, of course, thoroughly Malayan, producing pepper, maize, rice, sago, yams, cotton, opium, delicious fruits, such as mangosteens and durians; fine woods, as iron-wood, sandal-wood, and ebony; rattans, cassia, the gutta-percha tree, camphor, benzoin, cajeput oil, indigo, &c. Pepper is also produced.

The most remarkable feature in the Zoology of Borneo is the absence or rarity of many large animals, found in the adjacent islands. Thus, the tiger and the leopard of Java and Sumatra are unknown, their place being supplied by a smaller species, the *Felis Macroscelis*. Hardly less remarkable is the absence of both the elephant and rhinoceros from by far the greater part of the country. The most interesting of the large animals are the orang-outang (next to the gorilla the largest living ape), the wild cattle, and the proboscis monkey. Squirrels, deer, and wild swine are throughout most abundant.

In its birds, this island agrees very closely with Sumatra, the peacock being absent, while the argus and fire-backed pheasants abound.

HISTORY.

The growth of European influence in Borneo has been less steady and more intermittent than was the case in the Straits or in Java.

The Europeans who first visited this island, early in the 16th century were LORENZO DE GOMEZ in 1518, and PIGAFETTA, with the ships of MAGELLAN's expedition, in 1521. Both named it Brunei, from the port and principal town on its N.W. shores, at which, taking the most open course, they happened to touch. This name, written by the Malays themselves *Bruni* or *Burni*, is obviously the Sanskrit *Bharni* or *Bhoorni*, ("land"). Its conversion into Borneo, and its application to the whole island, came into use among Europeans in the 17th century. Some writers have stated that the island, in its whole extent, is called by the natives *Tanah Kélamantan*. The Malays, in the Dutch portions of the island especially, use this name. But those who have had more intercourse with the native tribes of Borneo, deny that they have, or ever had, any general name for the whole island. Commercial relations were soon formed with the natives by the Portuguese traders, at first in the city of Brûnei itself, and then in various other maritime States. In 1573 their Spanish rivals, who had recently established themselves in Manila, tried to open a connection with Brûnei, whose Sultan solicited their aid, and was reinstated by them in 1580. From that time the Spanish kept up intercourse with the country; but it was not unfrequently interrupted by war. The real influence exerted by either Portuguese or Spaniards was very slight; and the only missionary effort of which we have record in the 16th century, came to an untimely end in the death of the Theatine Monk, ANTONIO VINTIMIGLI, who had been its originator. Early in the 17th century the Dutch and English began to gain a footing in the island. In 1604 we hear of their traders on the West Coast, and in 1608 SAMUEL BLOMMAERT was appointed Dutch resident in Landak and Sukadana. The English visited Borneo for the first time about 1609, and in 1698 had a factory at Banjer-Masin. From this they were expelled by the influence of the Dutch, who, about 1733, obtained a monopoly of the trade. The Dutch power became predominant all round the West and South coasts, when the Râja of Bantam ceded his rights of suzerainty to their Company. The attention of the English was, in the latter part of the 18th century, turned to the North of the island, which was subject to the Sultan of Sulu, from whom, in 1756, ALEX. DALRYMPLE had obtained formal possession of the island of Balambangan, and all the north-eastern promontory. A military post was established there after the taking of Manila in 1763 : but in 1775 it was surprised and destroyed by the natives under the datus or subordinate chiefs, who were dissatisfied with the cession of their territory. The Dutch, too, were overtaken, in spite of apparent progress, with a succession of misfortunes, through their own mismanagement ; and in 1809 their Settlements were all abandoned by order of Marshal DAENDELS. The natives along the coast, assisted and stimulated by immigrants from the neighbouring islands to the North, had reverted more and more to piracy, and rendered the trade of civilised nations almost impossible, so much so that the Settlement which the English East India Company again made in 1804 was abruptly abandoned within a few weeks. In 1811, however, an embassy was sent to the British Government, then established in Java, by the Sultan of Banjer-Masin to beg their assistance, and a Commander and Resident. An expedition was then sent against Sambas, and a post established at Pontianak. On the restoration of the Dutch possessions in 1818, all these arrangements were cancelled, and until 1842 a free and undisputed field was left to the enterprise of the Dutch Government. A succession of active Commissioners soon laid the foundation of an extensive supremacy. About half of the kingdom of Banjer-Masin was surrendered by the Sultan in 1823, and further concessions were granted by his son in 1825. On the East coast also the Sultan of Kutei acknowledged for a time the Dutch authority. Then came a relapse: their authority was repudiated, and the troubles in Java diverted their attention from Borneo. On the opening of Singapore, almost all the Bugis trade, which had formerly centred in Amboyna, went there, and direct trade was opened with Sarâwak and . Brûnei. It became a matter of moment to the English merchants at

Singapore that piracy should be suppressed, and Mr. Brooke's efforts, upon making Singapore his head-quarters, were so warmly supported by them that he at last succeeded in procuring the assistance of English ships of war in this object. This led to political intervention; and in 1846-7 the Sultan of Brûnei ceded Labuan, and agreed to make no cession of territory to any nation or individual without British consent. The advance of the Dutch was thus checked, but this only increased their activity on the South and East coasts. In 1844 the Sultan of Kutci had acknowledged their protectorate and the area of their administration around those coasts has constantly increased. At the present time, they have a nominal suzerainty over two-thirds of the island; of which, however, scarcely one-tenth can be said to be actually under their control or influence. The English claims have always been confined to the North and North-east coasts.

CHAPTER VII.

A BRIEF ACCOUNT OF THE PRINCIPAL PLACES ADJACENT TO THE PENINSULA.

The following places are those with which the Colony of the Straits Settlements has its principal commercial relations :—

FRENCH COCHIN-CHINA.

Saigon, some miles up a branch of the Estuary of the great River Mekong, called the Donnaï, is the capital of the French possessions and protectorates in Indo-China. It was previously a place of small importance, although considered the second town of the ancient kingdom of Kamboja (Cambodia). From time immemorial, Kamboja, and especially this portion of it called Champa (Tsiampa), has been connected with the Malay Peninsula, and partly settled by a Malayan people. Saigon was taken possession of by the French in 1862, and since then has been placed in special communication with Singapore through the fine French Mail Service, and by the development of a considerable trade in rice, which is chiefly in the hands of the Chinese, mostly from Singapore, to which Port belong the six local steamers that ply there.

The six Provinces of Saigon are Bien-Hoa, Mytho, Gia-Dinh, Vinlong, Chau-doc, and Ha-tien. Area, 21,630 square miles. The population of French Cochin-China (1880) is 1,597,013.

SIAM.

Bangkok, is the capital and metropolis of Siam, situated on both sides of the Menam, about 20 miles from the sea. Population said to amount to 400,000. Bangkok is, to a peculiar extent, the centre of trade in the kingdom, of which it is the Capital; the principal articles being sugar, pepper and rice. A good deal of the sugar and rice is exported to Singapore, which may be considered to be the commercial metropolis for Siam. Frequent and regular steam communication now exists between the two ports. The opening up of Bangkok was one of the first fruits of the prosperity of Singapore. In 1826, the first treaty was made, but the great advance dates from the second treaty of 1856.

BRITISH BURMA.

Rangoon is thirty miles up the Irawadi on the East side of the river. It is the capital of British Burma, and has extensive trade in rice and timber, a small part of which is imported to the Straits. Population, 134,176. The whole of British Burma now contains about 4,000,000 people. Rangoon was taken possession of during the second war of 1852, when Pegu in the centre was added to our Burmese possessions of Arakan in the North and Tenasserim in the South. Rangoon has had an exceptionally rapid rise.

Moulmein is the chief town of Tenasserim, about seventy miles down the coast, to the South of Rangoon. It is situated thirty miles up the river Salwin. Population (1881), 53,107 souls. The staple products are timber, rice and cotton : and, like Rangoon, it carries on a considerable trade with the Straits. It is celebrated for the precious stones, found in the interior. It was opened during the first Burmese war in 1825, and is one of our English possessions in British Burma.

SUMATRA.

The trade of Sumatra with which the Colony is most concerned is that of the pepper-districts in the North (Edi, Oleh-leh and Singkel) ; from these the trade finds its way to Penang. The tobacco-districts are in the East (Langkat, Deli and Serdang) ; and rice and other produce are brought from the ancient State of Palembang, in the South of Sumatra, to Singapore.

JAVA.

Batavia is the capital of all the Dutch East Indies, as well as of Java, and is a great seaport and trading place, connected by telegraph with Singapore the principal trading places are Cheribon, Samarang, Sourabaya, Tjilatjap (on the South), Bawian (Boyan) near Madura, a small but populous island from which Singapore receives one of its principal streams of population.

CELEBES.

Menado is the capital of the northern Peninsula : *Boni* in the middle is the country of the Bugis ; and Macassar on the western coast of the southern peninsula, facing the Sunda Sea, is the chief place in Celebes, and the depôt of trade with Java and Singapore.

THE MOLUCCAS.

Amboyna, is the capital. Banda and Ternate are under its administration.

THE PHILIPPINES.

Manila, on the West coast of Luzon, famous for sugar, hemp and tobacco, is the capital of the Spanish Philippines, and carries on an extensive trade, sending out these things as well as cigars and coffee, as far as Britain and the United States. Ilo-Ilo on the island of Panay, is the second sea-port of the group and is the outlet of the best hemp-growing district.

TIMOR.

Timor is divided into two possessions—Dutch and Portuguese. *Koepang*, a fine port, at the south-western extremity of the island, belongs to the Dutch. *Delli*, a sea-port on the North coast of Timor, is the chief place at which the Portuguese exercise the little authority they still possess in the Archipelago.

CHAPTER VIII.

OUTLINE HISTORY OF THE BRITISH CONNECTION WITH MALAYA.

No account of the Geography of the Malay Peninsula and Borneo can be considered complete which does not include some outline of the history of the British connection with Malaya.

The history of our Settlements there is, properly speaking, but the latest chapter in the general history of British intercourse with this region, now extending over 300 years, which may be divided into three periods, viz. :—

1. That of individual and trading ventures (1578-1684);
2. That of trading closely connected with the administration of the East India Company (1684-1762) :
3. That of more direct political and military intervention (since 1762).

A brief reference to each of these periods will best serve as preface to the history of the Colony.

The earliest dealings of our countrymen with Malaya were the isolated visits of the discoverers DRAKE (1578), CAVENDISH (1588), and LANCASTER's first voyage (1592), prior to the foundation of the East India Company. These visits of discovery were of a buccaneering rather than a commercial character, notwithstanding the Royal Letters of Recommendation and the special Commissions of JAMES LANCASTER, HENRY MIDDLETON, and Captain BEST. These so-called Envoys were, in point of fact, ship-owners and merchants sailing under the direct encouragement of the English Sovereign ; but without having, so far as is known, any other than commercial objects committed to them ; and certainly in this earliest period they did not succeed in obtaining any other than commercial results from their missions.

DRAKE, in the course of his famous voyage round the world, came from the East to the Moluccas and touched at Bantam (1578). He is believed to have been the first Englishman to visit Malaya. CAVENDISH followed the same course in 1588.

Captain LANCASTER's first voyage in the "Bonaventure," (1592), was probably the earliest English venture to Malaya, simply for trade, though privateering, in addition, was by no means abandoned by him or others for the next 20 years. His ship left Zanzibar in February, 1592, and never cast anchor again till June, when it reached the shelter of Penang (Pulau Pinang) "in a "very good harbour between three islands some five leagues from the maine " (apparently Telok Kumbar). Here it stayed till the end of August, to check scurvy, which carried off 26 of the crew. It is singular that the very first English trader to Malaya should have found his way direct to this little, out-of-the-way and uninhabited island, which was to play so important a part nearly 200 years after. He loaded chiefly with pepper, &c., taken from the Portuguese and Peguan vessels he plundered off Perak, at which place three of them are said to have "laden a cargo of pepper."

HOUTMAN's Dutch expedition to Bantam shortly afterwards (1594-8), and another about the same time from Flushing, of which our celebrated countryman JOHN DAVIS was Pilot, were the first out of Holland.

1578.

The report of Dr. THORNE of Seville, the notes of LANCASTER's voyage, and still more the accounts of HOUTMAN's profits, first convinced Englishmen of the great gains that were to be made in Malayan trade. The East India Company was in consequence formed (1600), with a charter for 15 years, afterwards extended, chiefly with the object of trading to Malaya; and a few months later, this Company sent out the same Captain (now Sir JAMES LANCASTER) as "Admiral" over four vessels, with DAVIS as Pilot. He made for the Nicobars and afterwards loaded with pepper and sent home two of his ships from Achin (1602), where he was very well received. With the other two he proceeded to Priauan and Bantam, and at the latter place established a regular factory the same year—six years after that set up by the Dutch. Large profits were made, and two other expeditions were despatched; the first under MIDDLETON, immediately after LANCASTER's return (1604), and another in 1607. From this time the voyages were at first annual, and then more frequent, until, in about 1615, after the 13th voyage, the practice of naming each voyage by its consecutive number was abandoned. It was not till the "3rd voyage" of 1607 that Captain HAWKINS visited Surat and the West Coast of India, being the first English trader to do so: though the Portuguese had then been established at Goa a century.

It was still later, not till 1612, that Captain HIPPON in the "Globe," (the 7th voyage) on his way to Malaya, first showed the English flag on the East coast of India, at Masulipatam; and at Petapoli, near the Dutch possession of Pulicat, he left some people to form a factory. Thus the English trade with Malaya had already made some advance before the East India Company commenced proceedings in India. Until Madras was erected into a separate Presidency in 1653, Bantam was the chief town of our Eastern possessions: having been established nearly forty years before Madras (1639).

Captain HIPPON's voyage of 1612 is not only the commencement of British Trade in the Bay of Bengal, but his journey is also of interest as the first made round the Malay Peninsula in an English ship. He is even said to have formed a factory at Patâni. This must have been in 1613; and until quite recently it was common to find on our English Maps this date, under the word "factory," at Patâni.

From Patâni he paid the first English visit to Siam; and Captain SARIS, his fellow voyager, made, about the same time, the first English journey to Japan.

In 1613 (the 10th voyage) Captain BEST, the founder of the Indian Marine, with two "armed" vessels, visited Achin. But the success he had just obtained over the Portuguese at Surat, and the treaty ratified by the Mogul, had already inaugurated a new era for the Company, which henceforth naturally devoted more attention to Indian than to Malayan affairs.

But up to this date the East India Company had, in accordance with its name and the terms of its charter, been engaged in Malayan trade only.

At the time when these Englishmen appeared on the scene, they had been preceded by the Portuguese as conquerors, or settlers, in Malacca and elsewhere (1511); by the Spanish in the Manilas (1565-1571); by the Dutch in Bantam (1596), Amboyna (1605), the Moluccas (1607), and Timor Kupang (1613), which they had wrested from the Portuguese. [Batavia was occupied (1619), and later still Banda (1627), and Padang (1660). No permanent factories had, before this last date, been established in Sumatra, Borneo, or on the East Coast of the Malay Peninsula, except that above referred to at Patâni (1613), and those at Tiku (1615) and at Indragiri (1620), all of which were already abandoned. On the Malacca side of the Peninsula, it is true, the Dutch had, at this time, opened factories in Pêrak, Kêdah and Junk Ceylon; but that of Pêrak, which was established in 1650, was cut off in 1051, and in 1001 finally abandoned, until the Dutch, during the latter years of their rule at Malacca, re-opened it. That of Junk Ceylon was cut off in 1658, and that of Kĕdah was soon abandoned.]

After 1613 the British trade with Malaya may be considered established; and the practice of pillaging other traders was, for the most part, discontinued, here as elsewhere; but during the whole of this first period (1578-1684), our trading in Malaya, unlike that of the Dutch and Portuguese, and of our own countrymen in India, consisted in great part of individual enterprises of a non-political character. These enterprises were almost wholly concerned with the pepper trade in Bantam, and the spice trade in Banda, Amboyna, Ternate and Tidore. These were the local names then most familiar in England. and are to be found in MILTON's "Paradise Lost," in DRYDEN, &c.

There were also "private" ventures to other places on the coast of Sumatra for pepper, and to the northern parts of the Peninsula for tin and pepper. The English E. I. Company, though it did not promote them, and before long began to oppose them, as "interlopers," took advantage of these enterprises in some cases; but after the "Presidency" passed to Madras, our political status in these parts was inferior to that of the older settlers—the Portuguese, Spaniards, and Dutch. When our Company's traders were admitted, as at Bantam and Amboyna, into a kind of alliance with the Dutch, it was always humiliating, even before the latter became paramount through the capture of Malacca by the allied Dutch and Achinese (1641). After that event, the Dutch supremacy was. of course, more exclusive. No satisfaction could be obtained. either before or after 1641, for the "Massacre of Amboyna" (1623), though the story excited some indignation in England for many years.

The next period (1684-1762) is one of mixed commercial and political intercourse, promoted, and, as far as possible, monopolised, by the East India Company,—commerce being still first and foremost in the consideration of all, both at home and abroad.

The long Naval Wars with the Dutch, which terminated in 1674, were looked upon with little satisfaction in England; but they undoubtedly mark the beginning of an improved position for our Company's merchants in Malaya. The Dutch no longer succeeded when they tried against them at Bantam (1683) the same sort of opposition which had been so successful at Amboyna. Our merchants did not, on being expelled from the former, yield up the pepper-trade, as they had been ousted from the clove-trade; on the contrary, the East India Company's Government at Madras took the first opportunity to establish new forts and factories in Indrapore (1684) and Fort York at Bencoolen (1685). The former Settlement did not long continue, but that in Bencoolen was afterwards strengthened and secured by a stronger Fort, named after the great MARLBOROUGH (1714); and Bencoolen may thus be considered to be the germ of all our subsequent growth in these parts.

Other experimental establishments were also made at Achin (1666 and 1695), Jambi, Tapanuli, Natal (1752), Moco-Moco, &c., but none of them proved permanent. After the establishment of Fort York in 1686 all the Sumatran Settlements were made subordinate to Bencoolen.

1684.

The latest of the three divisions, into which our History falls, comprising the period since 1762, is chiefly composed of political and military proceedings, commencing with the Bengal Government's expedition against Manila (1762), and continuing down to the present time.

1762.

The result of that expedition was that the Spanish possessions were captured without difficulty, but were restored at the Peace of Paris (1763), when our possessions in Sumatra were also secured to us.

The only token of success retained by the English was the island of Balambangan, which was ceded by the Sultan of Sulu in gratitude for his release from Spanish captivity on the taking of Manila. This island lies off Marudu Bay in North Borneo, and is interesting as being. together with Labuan, which was then occupied for a still shorter period, our first acquisition of territory in Bornean waters. It was cut off by Lanun Pirates in 1774, and after being re-established for a few weeks by Lord WELLESLEY in 1804, was finally abandoned as unhealthy the same year: the fleet that took the Resident FARQUHAR there, bringing him away again.

The most important result was the familiarising of the Bengal merchants with this part of the world, consequent on the Manila expedition, and on the negotiations that followed at the Peace; and after the Treaty of 1763, Fort Marlborough (Bencoolen) was formed into an independent Presidency, which arrangement lasted till 1802. In 1781, Padang and the other Sumatran Settlements of the Dutch, with whom England had gone to war upon their recognition of American Independence, were seized by a military expedition from Bencoolen. This British ascendancy in the northern part of Malaya fostered the enterprises Captain LIGHT had for some time been carrying on at the time the settlement on Pulau Pinang was first projected (1786). That political motives and objects were not wanting is clear from the Treaty with Kedah, and the correspondence that preceded it, and particularly from the interest WARREN HASTINGS took in Penang's foundation. The Settlement was made in 1786 by friendly cession and payment. In 1796 it became the Penal Station for Bengal, in place of Port Blair. In 1797-8 a second expedition against Manila was fitted out from Madras by Sir J. SHORE, under the command of Colonel WELLESLEY. It was recalled before it left Penang. A full account of the island at that time, written by its Commander to his brother, who had become Governor-General. is to be found in " The Wellington Despatches" (Supplementary Despatches, Vol. 1., p. 25).

The history of this latest period of the British connection with Malaya is, in fact, speaking generally, the history of enterprises in which the Government, actuated by political considerations, has taken the lead in promoting British progress in these regions. There are certainly two recent exceptions to be made, in Borneo, of enterprises which bear something of the earlier private character, viz. :—Mr. BROOKE's action in Sarawak (1840-6). and Mr. DENT's more recent enterprise in Sabah (1880) But the general character of the period is seen in the two Manila expeditions—the successful one of 1762, and the abortive one of 1797 ; in the occupation, and subsequent recapture of Balambangan (1775-1804) ; in the foundation of Penang (1786), after some years of negotiation both in Bengal and Kedah : in the Marine Surveys of McCLUER and HAYES (1790-93) during the peace, and in the seizure of Malacca and of the Moluccas, as soon as the great War began (1795-1801) ; and again of Java, &c. in the later stages of our struggle with NAPOLEON (1811-14) ; in the foundation and support of Singapore (1819) : and in the protection (since withdrawn) afforded to Acain (1819), and the States of the Malay Peninsula, with which Treaties have from time to time been entered into, particularly during that unsettled period (1818-24).

There are three principal dates in this interval :—1805, 1827, and 1867.

The first of these brings to a close the period in which no regular English administration had been organised in Penang : affairs were managed by commercial Superintendents, and the Indian Government was content to leave their Malayan factories and possessions, in Penang at all events, outside the Indian political system.

The next stage exhibits an entire change. The Indian Government went from one extreme to the other. The rapid progress of the new Settlement's commerce at Penang was duly appreciated by the Government of Lord WEL. LESLEY, the early prosperity of the place supporting his views regarding "private trade;" as the Penal Station of India, it became of interest after 1796; the place was also brought to notice in the expeditions to seize Malacca (1795) and the Moluccas (1796); and that projected in 1797 against Manila; and a few years later by the capture of Celebes and Ternate after a siege in 1801 by the same fleet. These conquests were restored at the Peace of Amiens in 1802. But they doubtless caused enquiry, when quieter times followed, into Penang's political prospects, and the Malayan trade. Exaggerated notions then came to be entertained of the new Settlement's importance for naval and political purposes; and in 1801-5 the East India Company decided to confer upon it an independent Government, and sent out a Governor and Council, Secretary, Assistant Secretary and several Writers, after the fashion of the older Presidencies, with which Penang was now to rank. A Recorder's Court followed (1807), and enquiry was even made as to the desirability of abandoning Malacca (1808), the better to secure Penang's position. Then came the Java expedition (1811). Its large fleet and army, and its 900 killed and wounded, seem to have attracted much attention even in those stirring times. From this point the old commercial struggle with the Dutch also entered into the political phase: not so much through the temporary occupation of their possessions, as in consequence of the great political stroke of abolishing monopoly (1813), which followed shortly after our occupation. What Lord MINTO took in 1811, was restored: even Banca, with its Fort Nugent and Minto Town, which had never been Dutch at all, but was as much a British Settlement as Penang. However, Lord HASTINGS was ready to support Sir T. STAMFORD RAFFLES, upon whom his predecessor had relied, and who had governed Java for three years; and he allowed RAFFLES to found Singapore (1819), for objects adverse to Dutch monopoly, which are very clearly explained in one of RAFFLES's earliest letters from Singapore, dated June 10th, 1819 (preserved in the Raffles Museum).

Even the Penang Government was alive to the importance of preventing any re-establishment of Dutch monopoly at this crisis; and for that purpose entered into negotiations, which will be found recorded in the earliest of our Treaties with Pérak and Selángor (1818).

Soon after Malacca was finally ceded to us by the Dutch (1825); and when the shiftings and changes thus came to an end, the numerous experiments which had been made resulted in the existing form of united Colony, as finally settled in person by Lord W. BENTINCK (1827).

The next period is one of 40 years (1827 to 1867), in which the Colony remained a Indian dependency, but was left to develop quietly upon its own resources, with some pecuniary aid, though on a more economical scale than formerly, from the Indian Government; nor has any great break been made by the transfer, under Act of Parliament, to Colonial Office rule in April, 1867; which, though a momentous change, well deserving of the trouble that was taken in bringing it about, has not disturbed the continuity of our recent history.

1805.

1827.

1807-84.　The prosperity of the Colony since then, and the increased importance of its administration, comprising as it now does the three Native States taken under our protection in 1874, can be gathered from a comparison of the Revenues administered in the first year after the transfer (1868), the first year after the system of Protection (1875), and those now estimated for next year (1885) :—

	1868.	1875.	1885.
Singapore, ...	\$864,918	\$937,235	\$2,075,883
Penang, ...	324,196	453,029	1,264,170
Malacca, ...	112,725	118,307	308,215
Protected Native States—			
Pêrak, ...		270,000	1,650,334
Sělângor, ...		115,651	572.167
Sungei Ujong, ...		66,474	132,700
Total,...	\$1,301.839	\$1,990,696	\$6,003,259

The Census returns shew an increase in the population of the Colony alone, during about the same period, from 273,000 (in 1866) to 423,384 (in 1881). On the basis of the increment during the last decennial period, the population increases about 16,500 annually, and must now stand at the lowest at 473,000 for the Colony; to which must be added about 165,000 for the three Protected States, making a total of 638,000 now under British administration.

MALACCA.

Malacca is one of the oldest European possessions in the East, having been taken from its Malay Sultan, MAHMUD SHAH, by the Portuguese under ALBUQUERQUE in 1511, to punish an attack upon his Lieutenant, SEQUEIRA, in 1509. It was held by them till 1641, when the Dutch, after several fruitless attempts, succeeded, with the help of the Achinese, in driving them out. The place remained under Dutch government till 25th August, 1795, when it was taken military possession of by the English. The Dutch Government was dissolved on December 4th of that year; and the English administration which took its place under Admiral MAISWARINO abolished the Dutch system of monopoly in the Straits, as RAFFLES afterwards did on a wider scale in 1813. Malacca was held by the English till 1818; at which date it was restored to the Dutch, in accordance with the Treaty of Vienna. It came finally into our hands under the Treaty with Holland, of March, 1824, in exchange for our Company's Settlement at Bencoolen, and other places on the West coast of Sumatra. By that Treaty it was also arranged that the Dutch should not again meddle with affairs, or have any settlement on the Malay Peninsula, the British Government agreeing, at the same time, to leave Sumatra to the Dutch, saving only Achin in the North, of which the independence was protected until the recent Treaty of 1872.

A few years after re-occupying Malacca, a small force of Sepoys had to proceed against Naning, the interior district of Malacca, in which Dutch sovereignty had apparently never been fully admitted. Our first expedition (1831) failed; the second (1832) succeeded. In 1833 a Treaty was made, settling the south-east boundary of the Settlement as at present. There has been no disturbance in any part of Malacca since the "Naning War."

When Malacca was taken possession of by the Portuguese in 1511, it was one of the grand entrepôts for the commerce of the East, and it so continued till the close of the 16th century ; but as the Portuguese and other European nations pushed further to the East, in the Archipelago and neighbouring countries, the trade of Malacca gradually declined ; and the place ceased to be of much consequence as a collecting centre, except for the trade of the Malayan Peninsula and the Island of Sumatra. This trade it retained, under Dutch rule, till the establishment of Penang in 1786 ; when, in the course of a few years, it became, what it has ever since been, a place of no commercial importance, but possessing some agricultural resources. Penang soon acquired most of the trade of the Malayan Peninsula and Sumatra, Borneo, the Celebes, and other places in the Archipelago, not reduced to mercantile subjection by the Dutch ; but soon after Singapore was established, Penang in its turn declined in importance, the greater part of the extensive Eastern trade being centred at Singapore. [Penang's local trade has, however, largely increased within the last few years in consequence of the increased prosperity of the extensive tin mines in Larut, Renoag, Junk Ceylon, the tobacco plantations on the East coast of Sumatra, &c.] The opening of Singapore in 1819 may be said to have accomplished, for the time being, the ruin of Malacca's commerce. To use RAFFLES's own words at the time, " the intermediate Station of Malacca, " although occupied by the Dutch, has been completely nullified."

It is common to speak of Malacca as a place which has made little progress. But it is forgotten how absolutely undeveloped it had remained until it passed into our hands. The following is the official account of Malacca given by the Admiral in 1795 :—

" Though situated in the most favourable way for uniting all the resources " of a rich country with an easy communication by sea to foreign markets, " Malacca now labours under every inconvenience that an island does, without " its advantages, and though it has adjoining a soil capable of yielding the " richest productions of every kind, and though under the dominion of an " European power for about 250 years, it remains, even to the foot of the lines " of the town, as wild and uncultivated as if there had never been a settlement " formed here ; and except by the small river that passes between the fort and " town, you cannot penetrate into the country in any direction, above a few " miles, nor is even this extent general, being confined to the roads that run " along the sea shore about two miles each way, and one that goes inland.

* * * *

" This extraordinary want of cultivation was said to be the consequence of the " restrictive policy of the Dutch Government of Batavia, who made a point of " discouraging it, in all their Settlements, the more effectually to render them " dependent on Java, where alone they promote cultivation and improvement, " and from whence they supply all the other Settlements, even with the com- " mon necessaries of life. "

The population and agricultural development of the country districts of Malacca have, however, been very considerably increased of late years, especially since roads have been made throughout the territory. The Revenue has, in the last ten years, increased in larger proportion than that of either Singapore or Penang.

PENANG.

Penang, was founded on the 17th July, 1786. Prince of Wales' Island as it was officially called, was ceded to Captain LIGHT, acting for the East India Company, by the Rája of Kědah in 1785, on the stipulation that the sum of 10,000 dollars for 8 years, afterwards modified in 1791 to 6,000 dollars in perpetuity, should be annually paid to the Rája of Kědah, as long as the British occupy the island. But a few years later (1791) the sum was raised to 10,000 dollars, which has since been paid. This was settled, when Penang's territory was extended; and in consequence of the prevalence of piracy on the shores of the mainland, opposite Penang, a strip of the coast of the main, now called Province Wellesley, was purchased from Kĕdah for 2,000 dollars *plus* this addition to the annuity. The strip extended from the Muda River to the Krian River, a distance of 35 miles. Since the Pangkor Treaty of 1874 it has been enlarged, as stated above; and since that Treaty, also, the Settlement has comprised the outlying dependency of Pangkor and the Dindings, under a Superintendent, which gives an addition of territory almost equalling the Province in extent.

Province Wellesley is in a high state of cultivation, when compared with the neighbouring territories. The chief articles cultivated are sugar, tapioca, paddy, and cocoa-nuts. In 1796, the climate of the Andamans having been found unhealthy, the Penal Settlement there was abandoned (until after the Mutiny of 1857) and its 700 convicts were transferred to Penang, which by that time had a population exceeding 20,000. In 1805 Penang was made a separate Presidency under the East India Company, of equal rank with Madras and Bombay. In 1826 Singapore and Malacca were incorporated with it under one Government, Penang still remaining the seat of Government. But in 1829 Penang was reduced from the rank of a Presidency, and in 1837 the seat of Government was transferred to Singapore. The revenue and trade of Penang have increased remarkably in the last fifteen years.

SINGAPORE

Singapore was occupied by Sir STAMFORD RAFFLES, acting under the authority of Lord HASTINGS, on the 6th February, 1819, by virtue of a Treaty with the Malayan princes of Johor. It was at first subordinate to Bencoolen in Sumatra, of which RAFFLES was then Lieut.-Governor; but in 1823 it was placed under the Government of Bengal. It was afterwards, in 1826, as above stated, incorporated with Penang and Malacca, and finally became the seat of Government (1837).

Its rapid progress was, at that time, unparalleled. On the 11th June, 1819, RAFFLES wrote home: "My new Colony thrives most rapidly. We have " not been established four months, and it has received an accession of popu- " lation exceeding 5,000, principally Chinese, and their number is daily in- " creasing."

Nor has it disappointed the expectations then formed of its future: both its general and local Trade and its Revenues having, for many years, exceeded that of all competitors.

THE PROTECTED NATIVE STATES.

The Protected States comprise three "Residencies," all on the western side of the Peninsula, between Province Wellesley and Malacca, viz.:—Pĕrak (August, 1874), Sĕlàngor and Sungei Ujong (December, 1874). An Assistant Resident was first appointed to Pĕrak immediately after the signature of the Pangkor Treaty (January 20th, 1874), and shortly after to Sĕlàngor also (June, 1874).

The anarchy prevailing in almost all the Native States of the Malay Peninsula, and especially in Pĕrak, had been, for some years prior to 1874, a source of disquiet to the Straits Settlements, and a hindrance to the growth of local trade. In the beginning of that year steps were taken by Sir ANDREW CLARKE to remedy this state of things by settling the affairs of Làrut and

Pérak in the Pangkor Treaty (20th January, 1874), and, later on in that year, by stationing British Residents in Pérak and Sélàngor, and in the small State of Sungei Ujong, to advise their rulers respecting the collection of revenue and general administration. With a view also to enable the British authorities to keep order and prevent smuggling in that part of the Peninsula a strip of land South of Province Wellesley, beyond the Krian river, of about 10 miles broad, was acquired as British territory; and also a small portion of territory on the mainland, opposite the island of Pangkor, which had previously been ceded to us, to suppress piracy and without any idea of settlement in a Treaty with Pérak of 1825.

Towards the end of 1875, Sir WILLIAM JERVOIS being then Governor, Mr. BIRCH, the first British Resident at Pérak, was murdered (2nd November, 1875), and a force sent to apprehend the murderers was resisted; and, about the same time, the Residency in Sungei Ujong was menaced by bodies of Malays from some of the States near Malacca. Troops were obtained from India and China, a naval brigade was landed, and Pérak was fully occupied (January, 1876). During the previous month a military and naval force had already driven the enemy from a strong stockaded position in the hills between Sri Mènanti and Sungei Ujong, and dispersed the malcontents in that neighbourhood. During these operations, Sélàngor remained quiet.

Those concerned in the murder of Mr. BIRCH were captured and punished, the Sultan and some of the Chiefs being banished. Peace and order have since been maintained in all the Western States, and, so far as is known, throughout the Peninsula: a remarkable contrast with the state of things prevailing so recently as 1873. On the cessation of hostilities in Pérak (which had throughout been on a very small scale) it was finally laid down in Lord CARNARVON's despatch of 1st June, 1876, that the Protected States, without being either directly annexed or governed by "Commissioners," might continue to receive assistance in their administration from British Officers styled "Residents." Since then, in Pérak, Sélàngor, and Sungei Ujong, Residents have been stationed uninterruptedly, and have not needed any Military support. They are assisted by a staff comprising both native and European officers, and it is their duty to aid the native rulers by advice, and to carry out the ordinary executive functions, which are delegated to them. Supreme authority in Pérak and Sélàngor is vested in the State Council, consisting, in each State, of the Malay Chief, the highest native authorities, and the principal British officials. The Residents are directly under the Governor of the Straits Settlements. It is admitted that great success has hitherto attended the development of Sir ANDREW CLARKE's experiment.